SYSTEMIC APPROACHES
TO TRAINING
IN CHILD PROTECTION

Other titles in the

Systemic Thinking and Practice Series

edited by David Campbell & Ros Draper
published and distributed by Karnac Books

SYSTEMIC APPROACHES TO TRAINING IN CHILD PROTECTION

Gerrilyn Smith

Foreword by
Danya Glaser

Introduction by
Michael Nunno & Patrick Tooman

Systemic Thinking and Practice Series

Series Editors
David Campbell & Ros Draper

London
KARNAC BOOKS

This edition first published in 1993 by
H. Karnac (Books) Ltd.
58 Gloucester Road
London SW7 4QY

British Library Cataloguing in Publication Data

Smith, Gerrilyn
    Systemic Approaches to Training in Child
    Protection. — (Systemic Thinking &
    Practice Series)
    I. Title   II. Series
    362.707

    ISBN 1–85575–019–8

Printed in Great Britain by BPCC Wheatons Ltd, Exeter

To Lee Bird who couldn't wait for this book to come out.
With Love.

"to the idea that you can produce by training
[a hero-innovator] who, loins girded with new
[knowledge and skills] will assault [the]
organisational fortress and institute changes . . .
at a stroke" whilst recognizing "that organizations
. . . eat hero-innovators for breakfast".
[Georgiades & Phillimore, 1975]

And so to lunch . . .

ACKNOWLEDGEMENTS

I would like to thank all the current and past members of the Steering Group for the Department of Health Postgraduate Training Programme in Child Sexual Abuse. In particular I would like to thank Rosemary Arkley from the Social Services Inspectorate, Department of Health, for her interest, enthusiasm, and commitment throughout the duration of the project; the Department of Health trainees who have helped me clarify my thinking in child protection and training issues, and who were prepared to be involved in such an idealistic and challenging training programme with no guarantee for professional advancement after completion; all the many participants on courses I have run for promoting my own curiosity and giving me the benefit of their experiences; to Sarah Borthwick who read the first draft and gave me useful feedback, encouragement, and support as a co-trainer; Helen Armstrong and the members of the Evaluation Panel at The Child Abuse Training Unit for the stimulating and constructive discussions on child protection training; and finally to Jenny Ashford for her administrative support for the Department of

Health Programme and for typing the manuscript, which affection-
ately became known as "The Curse" after a typographical error of
"The Course", which just goes to show that mistakes can sometimes
generate new perspectives on old ideas.

CONTENTS

EDITORS' FOREWORD

I t is clear from events over the past ten years that child protection cannot be done from the perspective of one agency representing one aspect of a child's life. Inquiries and reports make the point repeatedly that good child protection must be a comprehensive, integrated process, which involves many agencies working together to create a network of protection around a vulnerable child. Child protection is being understood more and more as a phenomenon related to the working of an agency and its relationship to other agencies. Likewise, the training of child protection workers must reflect this orientation. Training must enable workers to see child protection in its broader context; to see the way family, health, legal, and safety issues all interconnect around one child; and to see the way Social Services, Health, Police, and Education agencies can interact to provide the necessary network of child protection services.

Within the confines of this book, Gerrilyn Smith does several things that have not been done before. She analyses the functioning of the bodies responsible for monitoring child protection in Britain (the Area Child Protection Committees); she describes a multi-disciplinary training course in child sexual abuse; she discusses the impact that training has on an agency; and she describes several aspects of her training techniques, such as exercises, which have been successful on her many courses.

Throughout the book her observations are informed by systemic thinking and the ability to see the connections between the different components of the child protection system. Her writing, which is borne of many years' experience in this field, allows the reader to "step back", take a broader view, and understand different levels of meaning about this work. The reader is also invited to think about what training means for individuals, their agencies, and the national monitoring bodies.

Very little has been written so far about training in the child protection field, and, as editors, we are pleased to bring this book to the attention of both trainers and practitioners in this particular field. However, the discussions of designing context-based training should make the book interesting to trainers in many other areas of work. The reader will finish the book with a new understanding of child protection and also with specific ideas and techniques for designing and carrying out effective training courses.

David Campbell
Ros Draper
London
March, 1993

FOREWORD

Danya Glaser

Traditionally, education has been primarily concerned with content. The importance of the process of imparting the information and the absorption thereof has only been accorded recognition more recently. Training, as one process within the education context, has the very specific connotation of intending to equip the trainee with particular skills. For both trainer and trainee, the process of training might be regarded as a very circumscribed task with clear delineation of the requisite background information that is needed in order to carry out the task, modelling or demonstration of the particular skills, followed by supervised practice by the trainee.

Within the general field of child abuse and neglect, the more recent and, indeed, far more desirable notion of child protection has been introduced. However, protection conveys the distinct sense of a prospective activity, simplistically regarded as the prevention of abuse ever occurring in the first instance; this is termed primary prevention. Secondary prevention refers to the protection of those identified as particularly vulnerable. Tertiary prevention is the protection from further abuse of those already abused and limiting the damage caused by the abuse. For understandable reasons, within the particular area of sexual abuse, it is the latter form of child protection which is of the greatest relevance, since the secrecy surrounding child sexual abuse means that it is usually only recognized retrospectively.

As must be clear, professional tasks within the child protection field are exceedingly complex and interrelated, and thus not amenable to being regarded as a series of discreet, independent entities or actions. Yet, as Gerrilyn Smith points out, training in child protection has been advocated as the solution, if not panacea, to allay concerns about professional involvement in the area of child sexual abuse. It might be argued that neither "training" nor "protection" is an appropriate term for the intended purpose. Furthermore, the repeatedly exclusive targeting of "coal-face" workers as the agents for changes in child protection after the abuse has occurred might be regarded as an inadvertent form of mirroring society's critical attention meted out to many children, be they struggling to disclose abuse or responding antisocially as a result of inappropriate care or neglect. From such inauspicious beginnings springs a comprehensive, clear, and, most importantly, constructive critique of the process of training.

Whilst inadequately trained practitioners are indeed unlikely to be in a position to respond appropriately, Gerrilyn Smith is able to demonstrate how contextual factors often conspire to outweigh the potency of newly acquired skills, and how, in some circumstances, these latter may even become counterproductive.

The book takes as its starting point an extremely complex and sophisticated training scheme and, in the process of analysing some of its shortcomings, moves on to creatively disentangle both constituents and contexts of the training process in general. It makes explicit the often implicit hierarchical nature of organizations, which might only become evident by the changes that a lowly ranked individual may expose by returning after training. It suggests that for the sponsoring organization to reap the benefit of a member's newly acquired knowledge and skills, it has to be prepared for the change that it will itself consequently undergo. The book is thus timely and highly relevant to the generic and expanding training "industry".

This is a personal account seeking to distinguish, by examples within the book, between observation/experience and inference/ interpretation. Gerrilyn Smith draws attention to the attributes and actions of the trainer pointing, for instance, to the need for a close and direct contact between the trainer and the trainee's context when the trainee is sponsored by an organization. This is but one of many examples of the necessarily systemic nature of the process. A question arises here about the degree to which any trainer should become involved in attending to a trainee's particular work context, even when such trainees initiate the training of their own volition and financial resources and in their own time.

A central position is accorded in the book to both the crucial initial and the maintaining aspects of the trainer–trainee relationship. Using actual situations as illustration, the author points to pitfalls and offers some very practical suggestions as to how to enhance this interaction between the key participants during training. Gerrilyn Smith emphasizes the need for attention to detail as well as pattern.

In ending their classical paper, the (then) Milan group hypothesized about the relative importance of the process of therapeutic questioning and the content of the final message to the occurrence of change (Selvini-Palazzoli et al., 1980a). Although the major emphasis in this concise book is on process, the importance of content is not forgotten. Rather, the interplay and interdependence between content and process within training is repeatedly illustrated. Thus, gender and race are considered as both. Gerrilyn Smith suggests that the trainer needs to possess the sensitivity and flexibility to alter or modify the content of the training in the light of process issues that arise during the training, without losing sight of the ultimate aims of the exercise. In this systemic book, both wood and trees are seen.

April 1993

INTRODUCTION

Michael A. Nunno & Patrick Tooman

From the mid-1970s to the present time a marked increase in public attention has forced a sharpened debate among the social science, clinical, and legal communities on the subject of child sexual abuse. In the most optimistic scenario, one would hope that this sharpened professional and scientific debate would lead to an increased understanding of child sexual abuse and to more effective human services intervention strategies. This increased public interest and the subsequent social and scientific inquiry has often had the opposite effect. Social and court-appointed inquiries into what appears to be an ever-increasing phenomenon throughout the United Kingdom, the United States, and Canada have left professional organizations, clinical experts, the courts, and communities divided. Our usual optimism in the process of scientific inquiry to illuminate both the citizenry and the policy analyst is tarnished by the scepticism produced by headlines that read, on Monday evening, "Children Never Lie in Reporting Sex Abuse, Researchers Say", and on Tuesday, in the same newspaper, "Researchers Find Children Falsely Report Sex Abuse". Even the social work, psychology, and legal scholarly literature in the area of sexual abuse of children reflects this confusion, with the resulting chaos played out in the child welfare offices, mental health clinics, and courtrooms of America.

Two opposing ideological perspectives have developed within the scientific and professional community in North America that shape the sexual-abuse debate. The ideological perspectives encompass a fundamentally conservative philosophy advocating for individual freedom, personal responsibility, and family values. The conservative champions of individual freedom and family values define the problem of sexual abuse as less severe and less pervasive in our society. They point to major over-reporting of cases of sexual abuse due to strict reporting laws, fear on the part of officials of repercussions if the report is subsequently found to be true, an increase in child custody battles, and fanatic feminists. While acknowledging sexual abuse within our society, they caution that the intervention of the child protective system may be part of the problem. Some argue that over-zealous investigators lead children into false accusations and further inflate the reporting statistics.

The second perspective includes child advocates and feminists who naturally support women's and children's rights. These advocates see sexual abuse as an epidemic in contemporary American society. They link its aetiology to institutionalized patriarchy in which women and children are the property of their husbands or fathers. In this regard child advocates and feminists view the sexual abuse of children beyond just the notion of incest. Sexual exploitation is present in all aspects of society's norms and values, and definitions of sexual abuse tend to be endemic in all aspects of society's institutions. They cite recent statistics that indicate that as much as twenty percent of the female population in the United States has had some unwanted sexual activity.

It is apparent the experts and social scientists from both ideologies have sought to use medicine, social science, and clinical expertise to unlock the secrets of child sexual abuse, often with less than precise means and outcomes. The deep divisions among experts existing on even the most fundamental questions, such as the frequency and definitions of child sexual abuse, provide the arena whereby the sixteen-year-old child's encounter with a "flasher" may be viewed with the same intensity as the eight-year-old girl's long-term sexual relationship with her father.

When Gerrilyn's publisher contacted us at the Family Life Development Center to write an Introduction to this book, the request was met with some scepticism that any human services "training book" would have relevance outside its home environment, let alone help illuminate the sexual abuse debate. Considering the normal scope of a book devoted to training and the differences in law, regulation, and "due process" that govern much of sexual abuse intervention within the United States and the United Kingdom, I felt my scepticism justified.

However, *Systemic Approach to Training in Child Protection* contributes to the scientific and ideological debate and illuminates the trainer practitioner in the process. It does this by recognizing that human services training, from needs assessment to program design to trainer delivery, is not built solely on enlightened and scientific theory but rather on the *ideological systems and values* of the sponsoring organization, the participants, and the trainer. The book approaches the meta-issues that support helpful learning experiences and relevant training. The book's themes focus the reader on the essential work of training—the dynamic interaction among the trainer, the participant, *and* their organizational affiliations. It addresses context-related learning with a clear feminist ideology by examining power and authority in the development and delivery of training for social services staff. Who sets the context for learning—the worker, the organization, the trainer, or is it a combination of factors that determines the product? Finally, the limits to training within any organization or community human services system are examined. Although the book's importance is within these broad contexts, it uses highly relevant case examples as its basic teaching points. The case examples illustrate a wide range of training issues, from organizational barriers to effective training to specific training challenges facing the trainer within the classroom.

Peter Senge's book *The Fifth Discipline* (1990) has popularized the notion of the learning organization. According to Senge, principles of shared vision, personal mastery, mental models, team work, and systemic thinking are necessary for effective organizational development within our complex society. Gerrilyn Smith's book places training within this paradigm. She speaks of a shared ideological vision, building a strong commitment to families and children, using teams as the primary vehicle for intervention and eventual treatment. Through training she encourages social agencies involved in sexual abuse cases (as well as the training participants) to find a sense of an interconnectedness or a system's view of their own organization, its work, and its role in the larger child welfare community. This is effectively demonstrated by the author's focus on boundaries, hierarchies, decision-making and feedback mechanisms, conflict resolution patterns, and the concept of strategic interventions.

Complementing this learning organization perspective is Gerrilyn Smith's strong position regarding the qualities and qualifications of trainers. She endorses a model in which the trainer remains a practitioner connected to the reality of the effects of intervention in the lives of families and children. Further, she elaborates that trainers must have an in-depth understanding of the work being done by training participants, and of the normal stress that is generated by effective training that demands that participants move to new levels of practice skill and insight. She illustrates common exercises used in many training programs that are designed to decrease anxiety but may have the opposite effect—for example, the use of experiential techniques pulled from a therapeutic context and placed into the training room can be confusing and may ultimately have counter-productive or even dangerous consequences for the participant. This is indeed an important message for all trainers. The author's systemic perspective on training is designed to encourage readers to renew their respect for the training process, as well as the organizational context that can affect group learning.

Gerrilyn Smith also recognizes the concrete and symbolic importance of the physical space where training is conducted. The training environment, and all the related services that support training, communicate the value the sponsoring organization has placed in the training effort. This may be a relatively simple observation, but the training environment continues to be overlooked by most public services training programs. A poor training environment will have negative effects even for well-designed training programs.

In summary, there is little doubt that the application of sound systems theory and adult learning principles have enhanced the effectiveness of our social services training. Without adequate training, professionals providing service to families and children can rarely reach beyond their initial skills. But training built on just good design principles, without clearly examining the ideology of the community's intervention system, can give professionals an incomplete picture. This book will help trainers examine their own ideological principles, and those of their programmes, for intervention in child sexual abuse.

June 1993

SYSTEMIC APPROACHES
TO TRAINING
IN CHILD PROTECTION

In search of charmed loops

T his book explores systemic approaches to training. The case material used is drawn primarily from child protection training. In part this is because of my experiences as a trainer, but also because child protection training, unlike many other types of training, attempts to bring together different professionals working cooperatively towards a common goal—protecting children.

Training is frequently the means by which working together is begun; the assumption that training together facilitates working together is also explored here. Additionally, the organizational structures created to coordinate child protection across agencies are discussed.

One of the major hypotheses to be made in this book is that training can be seen as a multi-levelled intervention into an organization(s). It can also be seen as a solution to dilemmas expressed at various levels within the wider system—the individual personal, the individual professional, the intra-organizational, the inter-organizational, and the supra-organizational. Training is viewed as an integral part of any organization and as one of the mechanisms by which an organization promotes stability and encourages differences. The balance between these two forces is critical to the integrity of any system. Too much or too little change will lead to unstable and ultimately dysfunctional systems. However, over time, like many solutions to dilemmas, training can itself start to become the problem, so, rather than producing desired change, it can inadvertently be inhibiting it.

The basic systemic concepts to be examined are:

(a)   co-evolving systems;
(b)   hypothesizing;
(c)   circularity.

These concepts are explained in a *Systemic Approach to Consultation* (Campbell, Draper, & Huffington, 1991). In addition to these basic concepts about systems, I explore other systemic ideas such as:

(d)   boundaries;
(e)   hierarchies;
(f)   feedback mechanisms;
(g)   executives within systems;
(h)   decision-making mechanisms;
(i)   conflict-resolution mechanisms;
(j)   engagement;
(k)   strategic interventions.

These concepts are discussed specifically in relation to training. A detailed description of these concepts is not provided, but it is hoped that the reader unfamiliar with these terms will glean their meaning from the context and application to the material.

The book begins by looking at the structure of Area Child Protection Committees (ACPCs) from a systemic point of view. Such committees are intended to provide any training in child protection in the United Kingdom with an organizational mandate. Additionally, the training subcommittee of an ACPC should have an overview of the training going on within the geographical boundaries of the local authority. ACPCs are deemed by the government the forum for interagency cooperation on child protection. Consequently we have a feedback loop that could theoretically travel from one individual worker through the lines of accountability up to central government and vice versa. This potential is rarely maximized or fully capitalized on. The direction seems to be more from central government through to the individual workers via official inquiries (see for example reviews of inquiries in: DHSS, 1982; DOH, 1991a, 1991b; or more detailed recent reviews of practice, as in the Cleveland Report, 1987). These inquiries are often activated by the practice of individuals or groups of individuals where the system has gone out of control.

One of the frequent recommendations of official inquiries is a call for more training. Unless the training can be tied effectively into the existing organizational structures and enhance the role-specific tasks of various employees in carrying out their organizational duties, it will in turn become a problem. This is a systemic concept where a solution to a problem is viewed over time as becoming a problem in itself, so rather than helping resolve the difficulties in working together to protect children it increases or perpetuates such difficulties. A systemic understanding of the function of training could enhance the overall functioning of an organization. Training could supply the executive system—or that part of the organization that is responsible for the organization's integrity and for inculcating new members—with a "snapshot" of different levels of the organization being trained. This snapshot would provide necessary feedback on the implementation of the policy, procedures, and practice that have been devised by the executive system of an organization.

After setting the widest organizational context in which child protection training should occur, I move on to hypothesize about various key aspects of training such as:

(a) selection of a trainer;

(b) selection of a course;

(c) selection of participants;

(d) engaging the training membership in the task of learning;

(e) using training materials as interventions for the course participants;

(f) facilitating positive transfer of training skills to the work context.

The practical material presented here is based on actual training experiences. However, details have been changed to preserve confidentiality. The practical material is meant to demonstrate pattern, so specific details are not as important as the patterns that emerge. It is hoped that the patterns will be familiar to other trainers and reflect training experiences outside the child protection field.

Whilst systemic thinking influences much of my practice, I will also be drawing on feminist theories that highlight the impact of race and gender in the establishment of dominant hierarchies. The idea of context-related learning will be a core assumption of the book. I am mindful that all training, but especially child protection training, occurs against a wider political-social context. Before moving on to explore the various aspects of context-related learning I would like to make a statement regarding my own value base, both as a clinician and as a trainer, and a summary of my core assumptions regarding child sexual abuse.

Feminists highlighted the issue of the abuse of power and authority in sexual abuse. Furthermore, feminist thinking made links between childhood experiences of sexual abuse and the rape of women (Kelly, 1988). The interplay of power, sex, and gender in the commission of sexually abusive acts has been confirmed by further research on convicted male sex offenders. Despite our knowledge regarding the role of power and authority in sexual abuse, there is still a reluctance to examine the wider implications that are implicit. Some clinicians have discussed mirroring, in the professional network, the pathology of the family (Furniss, 1983), but they have avoided a detailed examination of the authority structures of the child protection services and how they impact on both the individual service provider and the consumer (Morrison, 1990). A cursory look at the authority structures of agencies reveals an all too familiar picture of predominantly white men at the top, with predominantly white women delivering a service to a cultural mix of women and their children (Imber-Black, 1988). The exception to this in child sexual abuse is work with male sex offenders, where women as providers of the service are in the minority and the service is delivered almost exclusively to white men and boys—despite a continual need to emphasize the existence of female sex offenders—and ignores the needs of ethnic-minority sex offenders altogether (Smith, 1991). This continual need to emphasize the existence of

female sex offenders rather than generating real resources specifically designed for them minimizes the fact that the overwhelmingly
larger proportion of offenders are male. The same is true regarding
the ethnic minority sex offenders in that no specific programmes
have been designed to meet their specific needs. Child protection
work like any other type of work is carried out in a wider political
and social context. Yet unlike other types of work, it highlights
issues of gender and power in an uncomfortable and uncompromis-
ing way. Whilst issues of race and ethnicity are also apparent (often
more by omission), it is still the case regardless of cultural background that men sexually abuse women and children. In providing
child protection services this has major implications.

The needs of ethnic minority communities are not adequately met
across the whole range of services provided. Consequently, it
frequently falls to the voluntary sector to provide services that are
more relevant to particular groups. Whilst this is a pragmatic short-
term solution, it could lead to an abdication of responsibility by
statutory bodies for providing services to those groups.

Examining the authority structures of organizations involved in
child protection work demonstrates the lack of clarity surrounding
issues of accountability and responsibility, both of which are highly
relevant in child protection work. This lack of clarity directly affects
training because it is often training that is seen as the solution to
inadequate services (Cleveland Report, 1988; DHSS, 1982, p. 225;
Beckford Report, 1988; and, most recently, Warner, 1992). Hence
recommendations to deal with a shortfall in services often concentrate exclusively on training rather than on the resource
development of services. For example, professionals may be trained
to recognize the needs of ethnic-minority families in relation to
child protection, but not have access to resources for them. There
is already some evidence that by concentrating on training without
a concomitant investment in resources, this concentration inadvertently undermines the very training that has been provided.
For example, training teachers and nursery officers in a local
authority in recognizing possible indicators of sexual abuse led, not
surprisingly, to an increase in referrals to Social Services. This led to
a waiting list of unallocated cases requiring investigation because
there was no way the Social Services Department could cope with
the increase with its then current level of staffing. The waiting list of

unallocated cases attracted a high level of negative criticisms from central government, with no apparent understanding regarding the organizational shift in awareness that had resulted in increased referrals.

I have come to training in child protection by a circuitous route. I became involved in political action around sexual violence through the Women's Liberation Movement. It was the wider social context connected to my personal experiences as a woman that concentrated my thinking on sexual violence as one of the most potent idioms of oppression.

I was, at the same time, training as a clinical psychologist, in which there was little mention of gender, race, or sexual violence. I was a long way from home, an outsider, and so perhaps more open to new ideas and experiences than I might otherwise have been. This tension between the conservative orthodoxy of clinical psychology and the radical feminism of the London Rape Counselling and Research Project presented me with the dilemma of continuing a schizophrenic existence, splitting myself in two, or of forging bridges between these aspects of my experiences—synthesis or schism. My contact with systems thinking provided me with a conceptual vehicle that allowed integration of my seemingly unrelated experiences into one epistemological frame. It also taught me to look for patterns.

At first it was more themes that constantly emerged, areas of interest that I continually explored in many different settings: sexual violence, feminism, racism, therapy, power. This was the content, but I also became increasingly more concerned with process. What were the patterns? The use of authority and hierarchy as mediated by subordinate and dominant positions often defined by gender and/or race emerged as one of the most predominant.

This understanding impacted on my clinical practice first, which I felt most able to change. I had to read more widely and from different fields to continue to develop my interests. It is only more recently that feminism and family therapy have come together in articles in main-line academic journals, rather than being relegated to the fringe.

In June 1987, Rose Casswell (for the South West Region Women and Family Therapy Group) identified areas in training for develop-

ing a non-sexist family therapy. These were under the broad head-
ings of:

(a)   examining current family literature for sexist assumptions;

(b)   choosing to teach methods which are consistent with feminist
      thought;

(c)   ensuring that gender is the basis of any training programme;

(d)   using trainees' personal experiences to promote consciousness
      raising of feminist issues;

(e)   choosing a course structure that promotes politically aware
      practice.

The omission of race, especially in points (a) and (c), indicates
how much more consciousness raising was still needed by white
feminists to recognize and include racism within their conceptual
map of oppression.

Rose Casswell identified some issues in course structure that
needed to be attended to, such as struggling with issues of hierarchy
versus collectivity, challenging the superstar ideology, accountability and responsibility, and differentiation between person and role.
But oddly enough the comments on teaching methods focused
exclusively on teaching about therapy rather than about teaching
itself. Perhaps this reflects the fact that systemic thinking had yet to
be applied directly to teaching itself.

Systemic training, then, should attempt to make training a mutual process, it should foster the competence and independence of
the trainees, it should aim towards demystifying the training process by sharing power with the trainees, and it should demonstrate a
responsible exercise of authority conferred by greater knowledge or
status implied by the role trainer. Equally, one needs to recognize
that training interacts with wider systems and does not occur in a
vacuum.

I began to play with these ideas whilst in my second year of
The Advanced Family Therapy Training at the Tavistock Clinic,
London, where as part of the course requirement I had to teach
family therapy. Together with a colleague, Paula Boston, we inher-
ited a cohort of trainees and planned a family therapy course. We
regularly received supervision from Ros Draper, who introduced us
to the idea of hypothesizing about the training group (Boston &

Draper, 1985). I then began to see other groups I taught as systems. The members sat in the same seats week after week; you could predict who would speak first, who would have done their homework, who would ask what type of questions—patterns were emerging. I felt there must be a way that I could make better use of the material being presented. Equally I had to begin to ask myself, what was I doing that was the same? I was behaving like a teacher. I attended to content as best I could but I was not attending to process. It was not until much later that I began to look at the wider systems in which the child protection training I was offering was embedded.

I became convinced that if we are to intervene successfully in a system where sexual abuse has occurred, it is vital that the system from which we intervene (i.e. Social Services, Health, etc.) must demonstrate a respect for the responsible exercise of authority, a clarity of and respect for boundaries, a conflict-resolution mechanism, and a capacity to make decisions at the appropriate level in the organization, as well as an understanding of the issues involved in child sexual abuse. I found instead that the context of child protection work was one of overworked, under-resourced, and stressed professionals embedded in organizations that have different and sometimes idiosyncratic lines of accountability and responsibility, no conflict-resolution mechanisms, little understanding of boundaries, and a varied understanding of the issues involved coupled with the possibility of making executive decisions unilaterally and possibly impulsively in reaction to a perceived crisis. Cleveland (Cleveland Report, 1988), Rochdale (DOH SSI, 1990), and most recently Orkney (Clyde, 1992) all demonstrate the disastrous consequences of this state of affairs. Training is not the only answer. Whilst it may form part of a wider strategy to promote change and increase knowledge and expertise in a field, if it is isolated and disconnected from the contextual issues—such as the wider political perspective at the macro level but also the specific work experience at the micro level—it may fail to achieve any of its original aims.

Who is it, then, that sets the context for learning? The individual worker? The organization that sends the worker on the course? The trainer who offers the course? The wider social climate that indicated that more training was needed? A combination of all of these different levels/systems? A linear view of training cannot encompass all these complexities and different context markers.

Additionally, all the different levels involved in any one piece of training may not be consonant. A worker is likely to be experiencing dissonant messages. For example, the desire to train may come from individuals who wish to develop more expertise in running groups for sexually abused children. Their own agency may not wish to encourage them to do such a training, as there may be little scope to develop this type of work within the agency. Furthermore, it could conflict with the priority agenda of the agency, which might be to investigate allegations of child sexual abuse. On the other hand, the government may see post-protection work as the priority area of development. This reflects the potential range of dissonant messages any one individual may receive before even joining a course.

Cronen, Pearce, and Tomm (1985) developed a schema for a co-ordinated management of meaning. They identified a "charmed loop" as one in which no change of interpretation occurs regardless of which context is seen as higher in a hierarchical sense.

In the spirit of a true idealist, I live in search of the "charmed loop", believing that when all levels of the system involved in the protection of children can work together to provide a safe environment for the future generation then we will have achieved change of a higher order. In part, this is because I view child abuse, and in particular child sexual abuse, as isomorphic to the wider dominant ideologies that perpetuate and foster a culture of subordination and domination.

Child protection occurs at an idiopathic level and should be sustained by the wider organizational context within which it is embedded. Any challenge to the continuation of child sexual abuse in a sustained, organized, and multi-level fashion would be indicative, not only of a "charmed loop" (a multi-levelled consistency of meaning regarding child protection), but also of a paradigm shift away from institutionalized hatred and oppression that I believe dominate our society on every level of interaction.

The chapters that follow explore context-related learning by addressing both wider organizational issues, such as the structure of ACPCs, and specific exercises within training programmes.

Hypotheses regarding child protection services and other related systems will be generated on the basis of actual training experiences. A government-sponsored programme aimed directly at promoting organizational change within agencies will be outlined; many of the training experiences used in the book are taken from this programme.

The book does not intend to suggest a correct way to implement a training strategy but, more, to present a percolation of ideas from perhaps previously unrelated fields of training, systemic thinking, and feminism.

CHAPTER ONE

Do as I say, not as I do: disconnected patterns

AREA CHILD PROTECTION COMMITTEES: THE U.K. ORGANIZATIONAL CONTEXT

Area Child Protection Committees (ACPCs) provide the forum for joint working on child protection issues (DHSS, 1988) in the United Kingdom. Each ACPC must have representatives from the constituent agencies who play a role in child protection work. These are: Social Services, Police, Education, Health, Probation, and the National Society for the Prevention of Cruelty to Children (NSPCC) where appropriate. An ACPC is accountable to its constituent agencies, who are jointly responsible for the ACPC. Each member of an ACPC should be mandated to attend on behalf of their constituent agency and should have delegated authority defined to an agreed level by the constituent agency. *Working Together* recommends that the "level of decision making delegated to appointees needs to be considerable to enable ACPCs to operate effectively" (DHSS, 1988, p. 38).

Each ACPC should appoint a chairperson, who should be an officer of the Social Services Department of at least Assistant Director status. They should work to "written, agreed, terms of reference which set out the remit ... the level of decision which may be agreed by agencies' representatives without referral back to individual member agencies" (DHSS, 1988, p. 39). Each agency is encouraged to have a method of consultation with its employees to be able to monitor performance and identify policy, planning, and resource issues. A programme of work should be established to develop and review joint policies and procedures. There is a specific remit to review work related to inter-agency training.

With specific attention to the training role of an ACPC, joint training is recommended to "ensure a common understanding and thus foster good working relationships" (DHSS, 1988, p. 42). Induction training should ensure that all staff with direct involvement with children have an awareness of the indicators of abuse and understand local policies and procedures. Training is also seen as a vital part of making effective use of staff expertise.

Many ACPCs have a standing subcommittee that deals specifically with training issues. The recognition of the importance that training plays within any organization is reiterated in the more recent *Working Together* document (DOH, 1991b). An additional government publication, *Working With Child Sexual Abuse: Guidelines for Trainers and Managers in Social Services Departments* (1991a), has been published and is meant to be used in conjunction with *Working Together under the Children Act 1989* (DOH, 1991b).

This document (DOH, 1991a) provides guidelines for trainers and managers to develop a comprehensive training strategy for staff working with child sexual abuse. A comprehensive strategy is needed to "give the children and families the quality service they deserve and ... to recognise the considerable knowledge and skills required of [workers]. For a comprehensive strategy to be achieved, a strong corporate commitment is necessary" (DOH, 1991a, p. 2).

The training guidelines are divided into two parts. The first part lists seventeen points for consideration when designing a comprehensive training programme on child sexual abuse. The second part of the document provides a framework for implementing this training programme. Joint meetings with senior managers and training officers are recommended to review the implementation and development of training initiatives as well as linking them to an ACPC's overall training strategy. Another focus of these joint meetings is to explore other ways of developing knowledge and skills within the work context via good supervision of worker's practice, reinforcing material and ideas gained on training courses, and developing opportunities for staff to learn from each other through co-working (DOH, 1991a, p. 2).

These three documents (DHSS, 1988; DOH, 1991a, 1991b) form the core of government advice on the organizational structures that oversee the development of a comprehensive and strategic training programme in child protection.

SYSTEMIC COMMENTS ON THE ORGANIZATIONAL STRUCTURES

The existence of an ACPC as an overseeing body for developing, monitoring, and reviewing child protection services is extremely positive. It conveys a message from the highest level of social organization that working together is the only way we can move towards effectively protecting children from abuse. It also pushes agencies to find ways of facilitating inter-agency liaison both at the macro level of policy and procedures, and also—and more importantly—at the micro level of service delivery to the child and their family.

However, any guidance has to be vague, to allow for local interpretation within a general framework. Some of the tasks set for ACPCs are simple to write but extremely difficult to operationalize.

ACPCs are meant to function effectively as systems. They are horizontally organized, inter-organizational networks that are constrained by an administrative directive from a superordinate body, the government (Hallett & Birchall, 1992). They are large, continually shifting networks of coalitions and alliances (the latter are both familiar systemic terms).

The task for the executive subsystem within the confines of a system organized in such a fashion is extremely difficult. The government has mandated cooperation. This parallels the message "Be spontaneous" often referred to in family therapy. Mandated cooperation is a double message, implying an element of coercion in the mandate or directive juxtaposed with the antithesis of coercion—

cooperation. This can present the executive subsystem with a dilemma as to which part of the message it attends to—the directive process, or the cooperative aim?

As groups that meet habitually over time they will develop, of necessity, patterns of interaction and communication, and they will be subject to the rules that govern systems in general. The following systemic concepts will be examined in relation to ACPCs and their training subcommittee:

(a)   membership;

(b)   executive functions;

(c)   feedback mechanisms;

(d)   conflict resolution mechanisms;

(e)   decision-making mechanisms;

(f)   subsystems.

Membership

The government guidelines define membership and also suggest who should chair the committee.

Despite the helpful advice, membership can still be problematic. For example what is the optimal size of the group for it to function effectively? Does there need to be a quorum for decisions to be made? In large local authorities, other constituent agencies may not be co-terminous with the local authority; therefore, there will need to be several representatives from some constituent agencies. This will considerably increase the size of the committee. Some members who attend an ACPC do so because it forms part of their job description but this is not true for all members of ACPCs. How do members view attending an ACPC? Is it considered a high-status activity within their constituent agency, or just one task amongst many that they have to carry out? How long does someone serve as a member of an ACPC? If your performance is not adequate can you be replaced? How would this be done?

Membership is not static. Equally important, each member of an ACPC is also a member of another agency. How will loyalty conflicts be managed? If the ACPC meets quarterly, what is the likelihood that loyalty to the ACPC will override loyalty to the constituent agency for which the individual works on a daily basis?

In considering issues of race, gender, and class, it is obvious that the likelihood of a representative balance on ACPCs is small, given that membership is to be drawn from senior officers of constituent agencies. Because discrimination on the basis of race, gender, and class still operates, it will be some time before the senior officers appointed reflect the race and gender balance of the communities they offer a service to.

It is also interesting to note that in the list of recommended members to ACPCs, there is no mention of members of the community who would act as representatives of the consumers of the services. What implications might this have?

Executive functions

Government guidance is clear that appointees to an ACPC should have a degree of delegated power from their constituent agency so that the ACPC can make decisions without constantly referring back to the individual constituent agencies (DOH, 1991b, p. 6). However, clear guidance is not offered as to what that degree should be. An additional complication is that the chairperson has no executive power over other constituent agencies, which means that decisions require a consensus from all representative agencies before they can be agreed and then implemented.

Within any system the executive, frequently referred to as a dyad, has a responsibility to maintain the integrity of the whole system, to induct new members, to ensure smooth running, and to establish and maintain the boundaries of the system. This list of duties implies a greater degree of responsibility. Government guidelines suggest that the chairperson should be from Social Services with additional support and secretariat provided, the bulk of which should also come from Social Services. This conveys an implicit message regarding who constitutes the executive subsystem of an ACPC.

However, the role of the executive can be undermined if loyalties to the constituent agency of the members appointed to sit on an ACPC supersede that to the ACPC itself. If traditionally the executive functions of the system have rested with another constituent agency such as Health, then the handing over of executive functions needs to be dealt with clearly or acknowledged as being vested in someone other than the person recommended in government guidelines. If there have been long-standing conflicts between constituent agencies, these can then be played out at the ACPC. This is an example of where constituent agency issues supersede those of the higher context marker—the ACPC.

The executive subsystem of an ACPC has little control over membership and is obliged to accept appointees made by constituent agencies. By the same token, the members of an ACPC have little control over who is appointed as executive, and they are obliged to work with the designated senior officer from Social Services. This requires all members to trust in the constituent agencies involved to select appropriate members, to view the task similarly in terms of importance, and to respect the judgement of colleagues from different agencies—all prerequisites for working together effectively.

Feedback mechanism

Related to the above point, feedback mechanisms are an integral part of any system. ACPCs need to have feedback from each constituent agency. How the constituent agencies organize their consultation is left for them to decide. Additionally, if an ACPC has opted for a model of organization in which there are standing committees, feedback between the standing committees and the ACPC will also have to be worked out. Given the frequency of meetings, one can begin to calculate how long it would take for a piece of consultation work to go out from the ACPC to the workers and back to the ACPC. This can be termed the turn-around rate. The turnaround rate is calculated under ideal circumstances and assumes that an efficient feedback system within a constituent agency already exists.

Consequently, feedback mechanisms from the ACPC to the constituent agencies, and vice versa, need to be in place. Unfortunately, in the vast majority of child protection training I run, very few of the participants can identify their agency representative on the ACPC, let alone say what issues are currently being discussed. This indicates an absence of effective feedback mechanisms to individuals nominated onto child protection courses. It suggests that feedback within constituent agencies is minimal and not incorporated into the fabric of the organization. Consequently, the idea that practitioners might want their ACPCs to take note of specific practice dilemmas is quite alien. The necessary connection between service providers and policy makers is not being made effectively enough for it to be conveyed to someone outside the system—in this case a trainer.

Conflict-resolution mechanism

Many of these issues are intertwined. The need for a conflict-resolution mechanism is essential, especially as the constituent agencies, whilst being able to instruct their own members of staff, cannot instruct other constituent agency staff members. *Working Together* states that constituent agencies are "jointly responsible for ACPC actions" (DOH, 1991b) and that there should be "a clearly defined and agreed relationship between constituent agencies" (DHSS, 1988, p. 5). However, no guidelines are provided regarding what to do when there is a disagreement between constituent agencies. There may be an irreconcilable difference, which no amount of understanding regarding each others' respective roles will resolve. It could relate to philosophical differences or different interpretations of similar material. Whilst all constituent agencies in an ACPC may agree that protecting children is the common ground shared, there may be vast differences of opinion as to what constitutes the best way to protect children. This potential clash of epistemologies may be represented on the ACPC and then mirrored through the whole child-protection network. When constituent agencies within a professional network adopt rigid stances, about the best way to protect children, that are in opposition to each other, then experiences such as those in Cleveland that precipitated a judicial inquiry (Cleveland Report, 1988) are likely to arise.

In the absence of conflict-resolution mechanisms, ACPCs have little choice but to become conflict-regulating or conflict-avoiding systems. This means they will spend a disproportionate amount of time either regulating or avoiding conflict rather than getting on with the work they are required to do. Any task could activate the unresolved differences and block the effective functioning of the system. More and more work will be carried on either in subgroups of the ACPC or in the constituent agencies, independent of the multi-agency review.

The overall coordinating function will not exist and the possibility of cooperation and collaboration at the inter-organizational level will be unlikely to occur. This does not mean that cooperation or collaboration will not occur in specific cases with specific workers. This may occur in spite of differences being expressed at higher levels within organizations.

Decision-making mechanisms

If ACPCs had a clear decision-making mechanism, then conflict or differences of opinion could co-exist and not impede or block work from being done. The government guidelines offer no advice as to how decisions can be made. There is implied hierarchy in ACPCs by the strong direction for Social Services Departments to take the lead by providing a chairperson or vice-chairperson, the support services, and/or the secretariat. However, it is not clear if decisions then are to be made by the chairperson.

From my experience, it seems that decisions are made on the basis of consensus. After years of collective working, I was at first astonished, amazed, and then amused at the idea of ACPCs functioning as collectives, only able to move or decide on the issues that the whole membership agreed upon. Consensus decision making grants a right of veto to any member who does not agree. Systems that operate by consensus learn ways of being able to silence objectors, either by group pressure to capitulate to a majority-held view or by organizing the key discussion when the dissenter is not there. It is also an extremely time-consuming way of working. For consensus to work, the system must meet frequently and be able to discuss all points of view until an agreed view can be reached by the group. In its ideal it is meant to empower individuals to take a collective responsibility for joint action. It requires a high degree of commitment to the system by the members and a consensus within the system as to what constitutes the common ground or core consensus issues. Indeed, Paul Donnelly (1992) asserts that "a child protection decision making forum where consensus is the primary goal is dangerous" (p. 5). He goes on to say that "individuals are outperformed by groups only to the extent that productive conflict arises . . . and is resolved through balanced debate . . .". Given the structure of ACPCs, the frequency of their meetings, and the absence of both conflict-resolution and decision-making mechanisms, the likelihood of achieving a meaningful consensus is small.

Perceiving child sexual abuse as a public crisis facilitates a consensus that something must be done to prevent such an episode from happening again. Crises in child sexual abuse can, then, be viewed as necessary phenomena to secure inter-agency cooperation and collaboration in the public sector as well as to promote consensus decision making.

Subsystems

Many ACPCs have standing training committees to help co-ordinate a joint training strategy in child protection. The membership of the subcommittee, aims and objectives, and delineated tasks should all be set by the ACPC. The subcommittee should have clear communication with and be accountable to the ACPC. Consequently, many of the systemic issues raised previously apply to the training subgroup itself.

If ACPCs have many subgroups, this increases the complexity of the system and emphasizes the need for organizational structures that will facilitate working together. A training subgroup is an officially sanctioned subsystem. However, every ACPC will have subsystems that operate unofficially which may be more influential than those that are officially delegated to carry out the work. Issues regarding membership, frequency of meetings, and feedback to the superordinate authority of an ACPC will impact on the subgroup's effectiveness. As the training subgroup is the most relevant for the purposes of this book, its functions will be explored in more detail.

The primary task of a training subgroup is to facilitate negotiations for joint training, identify training needs, devise and plan a joint training strategy, and evaluate and review the training provision of the ACPC. This programme of work is outlined in more detail in *Working with Child Sexual Abuse* (DOH, 1991a).

Its task is made more complex by the way in which training is viewed, managed, and organized in different constituent agencies and across different disciplines. Identifying who should represent the child protection training needs of staff on the subgroup for any one constituent agency will be difficult.

There is a need to catalogue or conduct an inventory of the baseline level of training in child protection that any one discipline may have received whilst qualifying, before moving on to identify what training is offered by single agencies and between agencies.

The task of a training subgroup should remain essentially a mapping and prioritizing exercise. This includes identifying what should remain single-agency training, and what prerequisite learning would facilitate multi-agency training.

By using the training subgroup more effectively, the ACPC would then free time for overseeing the whole spectrum of child protection work. This requires a degree of delegation and the appointment of key training staff to such a subgroup. If the same people are on all the subgroups of the ACPC, it would be important for the ACPC to devise strategies for increasing its pool of expertise. The consequence of such overlapping membership would be that the context marker of the subgroup itself would become invisible. Consequently, the focus of the group—in this case on training— would be hard to maintain.

RECOMMENDATIONS
FOR ENHANCING ACPC FUNCTIONING

The preceding material summarizes some of the main organizational structures that oversee the delivery of child protection training in the United Kingdom. Structural difficulties at this level of an ACPC and its training subgroup will almost certainly produce training programmes that will be disconnected and dislocated from the organizational authority that implicitly underpins them. The consequences of this disconnection and dislocation can be very dysfunctional at every level and work against the common goal of protecting children from sexual abuse. The disconnected, dislocated line of authority in the organization will be unable to impact effectively on the perverted and damaged line of authority in the family in which sexual abuse has occurred.

There are some structural recommendations that can be made, based on systemic principles, that may promote more effective organizational functioning which ultimately should enhance child protection work. They can be summarized as follows:

(a)   An executive subsystem needs to be clearly identified and agreed by all constituent agencies.

(b)   The executive subsystem needs to be able to establish mechanisms whereby feedback can be obtained, conflicts resolved, and decisions made.

(c)   The process of establishing such structures is as important as the structures themselves.

(d)   The executive subsystem must be able to devise a structure, including officially sanctioned subsystems operating to an agreed level of delegated authority, that facilitates the work of the ACPC.

(e)   Membership both to the ACPC and to its subgroups should be clearly articulated. Strategic co-options should ensure that all agencies are represented and that the members of any subgroup can work together effectively towards a consensus view.

(f)   Each subgroup in turn needs to have an executive, usually a chairperson, who is accountable to the superordinate body of the ACPC and responsible to both the membership of the subgroup and the ACPC.

Additional consultations should be offered to ACPCs directly, perhaps focusing on conflict resolutions, feedback systems, and decision making. This could help to establish the common ground or domain consensus (Benson, 1975) that is a prerequisite of co-operation across different agencies. It would also increase the frequency of contact between members and help to establish a commitment to the ACPC system. To use training for the ACPC as a means of achieving this, as recommended by Ducanis and Golin (1979), perpetuates the notion that training is the answer to organizational problems. Offering systemic development consultations

(Campbell et al., 1991), rather than training, would help maintain the focus on human resources, the management of change in organizations, and the necessary interconnectedness between policy and practice, managers, and service providers and consumers.

These recommendations all highlight and emphasize how training is often used as a solution to the implementation gap between policy and practice. This training is often targeted to the least relevant audience—practitioners. Relevance here is measured in terms of those most able to promote the organizational change needed for the integration of policy, procedure, and practice issues to occur. Additionally, it demonstrates a request from one level in the multi-agency forum—the ACPC—to another level—the multi-disciplinary workers—to work together in a way that the higher level is unable to do itself: a classic example of "Do as I say, not as I do". A systemic approach to training could resolve some of these issues.

CHAPTER TWO

Training as a strategic intervention to an organization

This chapter outlines a training programme sponsored by a central government grant (Department of Health Post-graduate Training Programme in Child Sexual Abuse) that specifically aimed to promote organizational change in post-protection work in families where sexual abuse is an issue. Additionally, hypotheses are generated regarding how the course was consumed by the organizations who successfully nominated onto the programme. It is postulated that organizational styles will be reflected throughout the whole of the programme, from selection of the individual nominee to the implementation of the training component in the nominating authority. In this way, the training programme itself constitutes a strategic intervention to the ACPC and, hopefully, provides useful feedback to many levels within the child protection network.

The programme is comprised of four major components run over two years: an academic programme over an academic year focusing on policy and procedural issues, assessment of risk, treatment, and training issues; a clinical placement in a specialist centre over twelve months; organizational consultations to a Development

Group over two years; and training devised by that Development Group offered in the nominating authority over two years. This programme has a Steering Group which oversees the development and implementation of the programme itself. All component parts of the programme are represented on the Steering Group, which meets quarterly. There is a core membership from the Department of Health and the academic institution that runs the programme, with co-opted members from intakes representing different perspectives such as the trainee, the Development Group, the ACPC, and, most recently, voluntary organizations.

Applications are invited from experienced practitioners supported by their ACPCs to apply to the programme. Each successful nominee is required to have the backing of their ACPC and to establish a multi-disciplinary Development Group to facilitate and promote organizational change in the delivery of post protection services in child sexual abuse cases. This is an example of trying both to identify the path of "least organizational resistance" and to assemble a critical mass to facilitate change (Goergiades & Phillimore, 1975).

The programme was set up as a pilot project. There have been four intakes, each of which has been modified in light of feedback from previous intakes. Thus the course has a co-evolving structure. A summary of the programme intakes is included in the Appendix. The majority of candidates are white women from Social Services Departments; the number of health services personnel has reduced with each successive intake. The majority of constituency agency managers are white men.

Originally, the Development Groups had been called Support Groups. In the second intake, this was changed to Support Implementation Groups. By the third intake, the name had finally changed to Development Groups.

Initially, the trainee the core of each Development Group consisted of the trainee nominated to the programme, but, as the programme learned from itself, this was increased to include the trainee's Line Manager and a representative of the ACPC. Over each of the four intakes the involvement of the Development Group has increased from initially a hand-holding operation to a more active participation in almost all aspects of the programme itself.

It is now recommended that a Development Group should be multi-disciplinary, and that the members be drawn from different constituent agencies, represent a balance between managers and practitioners, and include the trainee, the trainee's Line Manager, a member of the ACPC, someone who has a training remit and sits on the training subcommittee of the ACPC, and, if possible, a representative from the Probation services. The average size of the Development Groups in the programme has increased with each successive intake, levelling off at approximately ten members.

Additionally, a second trainee attends the whole of the academic term on treatment issues. This should be a practitioner, preferably one who will continue to work with the lead trainee once they return to the nominating agency. For the first year, the lead trainee is out of the nominating authority two days per week; one day is for academic work, the other for the clinical placement. The idea of a second trainee was implemented in the fourth intake in response to feedback from previous intakes about the isolation that trainees felt in trying to put into practice the new ideas and clinical skills they had been exposed to on the programme.

The primary aim of the Development Groups is to enhance transfer of learning of the trainee to the widest possible audience within the organization. This is facilitated if Development Groups meet frequently, have a chairperson, and are committed to the programme. Members of a Development Group receive consultations from the Course Lecturer four times over the two years the programme is run. These are offered in conjunction with the Social Services Inspectorate, a government department concerned with promoting standards in child protection work. In addition, members of each Development Group are invited to attend workshops held at the end of each academic term, focusing on a particular theme. These have been:

(a)   policy issues (traditionally attended by managers and ACPC representatives);

(b)   organization of treatment services (attended by practitioners and their managers);

(c)   training issues (attended by those with a remit for training).

The trainee attends all workshops with members of their Development Group. In this way members of the Development Group access certain portions of the programme that are most relevant to the development of target services and to their professional role within the Development Group. It also helps to maintain the necessary cohesion the Development Group may need to continue with planned innovations in the face of organizational ennui or resistance (Georgiades & Phillimore, 1975).

Child-protection police colleagues attend two consecutive workshops on assessment of children's allegations. Training officers are also invited to attend an additional workshop in which the focus is to devise a training strategy to be implemented in the nominating authority. This training is done with the lead trainee and the Course Lecturer, and it should help to further the aims of the Development Group. Many of the training programmes referred to in this book come from these workshops.

At the workshops each of the nominating authorities has an opportunity to develop its own aims and objectives in relation to the workshop theme and to compare and comment on those of the other nominated authorities. Each intake has been small, the largest being the first which included nine nominating authorities.

Trainees from previous intakes are invited to continue in the programme, either by offering clinical placements or by teaching on the academic component. Networking is encouraged, both informally and through the workshops.

The perspective of the course is systemic in that it concentrates on the context issues impacting on the individual trainees and encourages them to hypothesize about their organizations and the services that can be realistically provided. Other theoretical models are specifically examined in the academic component and within the clinical placements themselves.

The cost of the course is borne by the Department of Health and the nominating authority. The nominating authority must release staff to attend relevant portions of the programme. For the lead trainee this is substantial (i.e. two days per week for a year). Travel costs vary, as applicants come from a wide geographical spread. These are borne by the nominating authority.

Each successful nominating authority is allocated four organizational consultations to the Development Group, five training workshops devised by the Development Group in service of its aims, as well as the clinical and academic component. The latter components happen away from the nominating authority, whilst the former take place within the nominating authority.

As the training component is primarily designed by the Development Group, its implementation (or not) is a good indicator of the effectiveness of the group's functioning in relation to the issue of positive transfer of training skills. A graph indicating the proportion of training days used by each nominating authority is presented in Figure 1. The first intake is not included, as this component of the programme had not been developed to this extent.

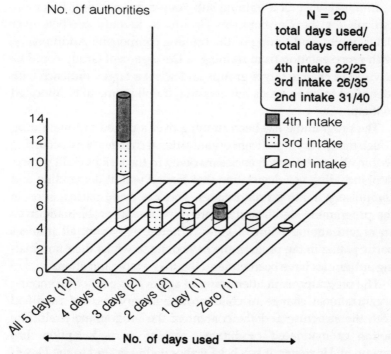

No. of authorities

N = 20
total days used/
total days offered

4th intake 22/25
3rd intake 26/35
2nd intake 31/40

■ 4th intake
⊡ 3rd intake
▱ 2nd intake

14
12
10
8
6
4
2
0

All 5 days (12)   4 days (2)   3 days (2)   2 days (2)   1 day (1)   Zero (1)

◄──────── No. of days used ────────►

The training component was not offered to the first intake. Five days per nominating authority were allocated to be implemented in the second twelve months of the programme

Figure 1:   Use of training days

The majority of nominating authorities manage to use the five training days. However, some do not. The most common reason given for not taking up the training is the lack of a connection with a training forum that will facilitate the administrative back-up to the training.

If the Development Groups are working effectively and have a representative from the training subcommittee, then the five training days can be included in the overall training strategy devised by the ACPC over the coming years. Unfortunately, despite appropriate representation, this rarely happens. The training is frequently offered in addition to the planned training rather than embedded within the overall training strategy. This has led to a range of difficulties such as poor attendance, double booking, and inappropriate target audiences, to name a few.

In the absence of a training subgroup representative, it is more difficult for the Development Groups to identify conflicts over dates, topics, and timing of the training component. Additionally, with representation from training, a Development Group could be advised to change target groups and select a target audience with identified training needs but awaiting training time to be allocated to them.

The programme has been running over a period of time during which many very significant organizational changes were occurring within all constituent agencies involved in the task of child protection, including new legislation that carried with it demanding and compulsory training programmes. This has made participation in the programme significantly more difficult and problematic from an organizational point of view. Without exception, all trainees participating in the programme have done so whilst their nominating authorities have been undergoing major reorganizations.

The programme, in attempting to achieve its goal of promoting organizational change in child protection services, has modified both the structure and the content of the programme itself. The notion of mandated candidates, present at its inception, has remained. However, it has been elaborated to extend to the Development Groups themselves, which in the most recent intake are often officially sanctioned, time-limited project subcommittees of the nominating ACPC.

There are still persistent unresolved difficulties with the course and its structure that mitigate against achieving its desired aim of organizational changes. These can be summarized as follows:

- *Target audience*. Identifying potential consumers of the course has been problematic. Is it the ACPC? The Development Groups? An agency? An individual? Whilst it is easier now to communicate directly with ACPCs via the chairperson, organizationally they are still unwieldy committees that lack executive decision-making power around the details of participation on such a programme. In the absence of an ACPC budget, the cost of participation falls heavily on the agency from which the lead trainee is seconded onto the programme. However, ACPCs could express a desire to participate, identify a service that needs to be developed locally in relation to post-protection services in child sexual abuse, and help to constitute a Development Group. Interest in the course for all intakes to date has come primarily from potential nominees, who then organize (more or less successfully) the necessary managerial and ACPC backing.

  Changing patterns of consumption of training, from individuals participating to Development Groups and/or agencies, is partially addressed by the requirement that each nominee must have a written letter of support from the ACPC prior to a place on the programme being offered. If a nominee is successful at interview then a letter of confirmation is sent to the ACPC detailing the necessity of a Development Group and outlining those aspects of the programme that will be delivered in the home agency and additional participation of relevant members of the Development Group.

- *Geographical accessibility and location*. The geographical location of the academic programme, and to a lesser extent the clinical placements (which are specialist centres throughout the southeast of England), prohibits some ACPCs from easily participating. The majority of participants come from the south of England, but certain regions have never nominated onto the programme. As a national initiative, this is unsatisfactory.

The Department of Health Programme is run by the Institute of Child Health in conjunction with the Hospital for Sick Children, known as Great Ormond Street. The hospital's reputation in the field of sexual abuse is renowned. Consequently, the venue for the Department of Health Programme at the Institute of Child Health is not a neutral one. In the independent evaluation carried out on the programme this was referred to by some of the past trainees. The high profile of the hospital was both a positive and negative factor. Some agencies positively selected the programme because of the connection; some positively avoided the programme because of the connection.

- *Course structure.* As the programme continues to evolve, it is moving further away from the notion of training one individual to do many things—a reticulist model (Hallett & Birchall, 1992)—to a more collective approach, encouraging a small number of professionals to work together towards a specific goal or service development.

  However, the bulk of the programme is still delivered by the Course Lecturer only, rather than by a multi-disciplinary team akin to the ones that exist in the clinical placements and which are encouraged in the formation of Development Groups. Consequently, the model of a single Course Lecturer that is presented inadvertently works against one of the main tenets of the programme, which is to promote cooperative working across disciplines and agencies. The course is thus modelling a reticulist approach in which an individual is seen as the agent of change.

  Hallett and Birchall (1992) describe the reticulist model and add this cautionary note: "While a reliance on reticulists may be appropriate or sufficient for the development of rare or innovative projects, it is insufficient for the more mundane, routine and widespread coordination required in each locality in the field of child protection" (p. 63).

- *Redeployment upon completion.* Once trainees have completed the programme, they have a wealth of new ideas and clinical and training skills that their current job may not encompass or promote. The flexibility of organizations to adapt job specifications to suit candidates that they have themselves seconded for further training is, ironically, limited. However, the degree to which the organization supported the nominee is often directly reflected in the efforts made to continue to employ them within the organization once the programme has been completed. At best, the nominee is already in a post that could make use of such additional knowledge and expertise (the minority of candidates); at the worst, the nominee is over-qualified and/or possesses new skills that are not relevant to the job they occupy and no other post is offered to them.

Despite these shortcomings, the programme is very successful in improving individual knowledge and clinical and training skills. It is less successful at promoting organizational change. Nonetheless, using systemic principles and the programme itself as an intervention, it is possible to hypothesize and design further interventions that will help organizations maintain the balance between too much change and too little change. The combination of organizational consultations to a Development Group, academic and clinical components offered to strategic professionals who are also members of the Development Group, and the implementation of a training programme devised in principle by the Development Group in service of developing specific aspects of child protection work, offers the possibility of creating change of a multi-levelled order rather than at the traditional level of an individual trainee.

The following chapters attempt to demonstrate how systemic ideas can be applied in a variety of training contexts. This should provide individual trainers with a greater degree of flexibility when training and encourage them to view the training itself as an intervention into an organization rather than a linear or unidirectional prescription to correct identified problems.

CHAPTER THREE

Generating systemic hypotheses from training experiences

This chapter uses actual training experiences to illustrate some of the theoretical material presented. Systemic thinking suggests that patterns will manifest themselves more easily to those who have a meta-perspective. Training experiences offer an ideal opportunity to develop the necessary distance from a work system to start reorganizing wider patterns that may be inhibiting or preventing certain changes from occurring despite an expressed policy perhaps promoting them.

It is postulated that hypotheses can be generated about the way services are delivered in any one particular area from the way that area organizes its ACPC. If organizational patterns are embedded throughout the organization and new members (i.e. employees) are inculcated into the system by the executive subsystem (i.e. managers) who have a responsibility for the induction of new members, and who are also part of the ACPC, then you would expect to be able to generate hypotheses about service delivery on the basis of the structure and style of the ACPC itself.

The examples used are taken from ACPCs who have successfully nominated candidates on to the Department of Health Postgraduate Training Programme in Child Sexual Abuse, which aims to promote organizational change through mandated nominees work-ing in conjunction with local Development Groups to develop specific assessment and treatment services for children and their families where sexual abuse is an issue.

Example 1

Local Authority A has a very large ACPC with good representation from all constituent agencies. The ACPC meets quarterly. It has six subcommittees, three of which are standing subcommittees—training, case review, and policy—and three of which are ad hoc, dealing with specific issues which include staff disciplinary matters following allegations of sexual abuse by staff, multi-lingual and multi-cultural issues in investigation of allegations of sexual abuse, and treatment issues. Decision making is by consensus. There are no conflict-resolution mechanisms. The feedback mechanism to members of Social Services staff is done by child protection workers who are strategically placed in each area office and hold regular debriefing meetings with staff following ACPC meetings.

The membership of each of the subcommittees is almost identical to that of the ACPC. The feedback between the ACPC and the subcommittees is not formalized, primarily because of the signifi-cant overlap in membership. There is no budget for the ACPC.

Possible hypotheses

(a)   The senior officers in some organizations find it difficult to delegate, hence the need to be on all committee subgroups as well as the main committee itself.

(b)   There is a high level of expressed or unexpressed conflict between constituent agencies, which requires attendance at all meetings by some senior members.

(c)   It is difficult to stay on task as context markers are unclear, with the individuals doing different tasks.

(d)   There is a lack of role differentiation, manifested by a belief that everybody needs to do everything and can do everything.

(e)   There is no conflict-resolution mechanism; consequently, differences must be denied and/or minimized.

These hypotheses could be tested out by offering consultation to the ACPC itself, or by setting tasks for a subgroup to complete. Based on the hypotheses generated, predictions could be made as to how and if the task would be undertaken. The design of the task itself would be an intervention to the organization. Additionally, predictions can be made as to how the ACPC would use the Department of Health Programme.

Significantly, the trainee nominated by this ACPC to attend the Department of Health Programme was embedded in a Social Services Area Team (i.e. at the bottom of the hierarchy). This illustrated the organizational belief of Social Services that all members of staff are equally able to influence the system. The Development Group—which consisted of the trainee, the Line Manager of the trainee, and an ACPC representative—had a membership that did not overlap with any other subgroup of the ACPC, save the ACPC representative, who left the authority mid-way through the programme and was not replaced on the Development Group despite being replaced in the authority. The Development Group did not function. It met rarely and was unsuccessful in establishing any organizational changes, unable to agree on a training strategy or to implement the training strategy the trainee had designed for the nominating authority.

Given the structure of the ACPC and its subgroups, it is clear that the Development Group's constitution was too novel a collection of individual workers to effect organizational change successfully. Additionally, whilst the nomination was made by consensus, it would appear that some key players did not fully agree with the nomination but were not prepared to dissent openly when it was discussed at ACPC level.

The selection of the candidate and the subsequent use of the programme seems to reflect the organizational style, identified from the way in which the ACPC organized itself. At final follow-up the trainee attended with a Child Protection Officer who was formerly the Line Manager and who was about to leave Authority A. This was a visible demonstration of the lack of:

(a)   organizational support for the nomination;

(b)   role definition, as the worker about to leave Authority A represented the Development Group, the Line Manager, and the ACPC simultaneously.

The training offered in this case did not generate positive transfer of skills into the nominating authority, nor did it function as an intervention into the organizational system that successfully maintained its boundaries from outside influences. The intra-agency conflict it generated was so great that none of the training days offered was implemented. Conflict or differences of opinion resulted in system paralysis and a total inability to act as a system, leaving the individual trainee isolated, undervalued, under-used, and under-employed, with her training experience remaining a personal, professional development.

Example 2

Local Authority B has a very small executive ACPC with a larger number of professional advisers. Each member of the executive has delegated authority from their constituent agency to a defined and explicit level. The ACPC is serviced by a secretariat that is partially funded by the ACPC itself from the budget it has organized.

There are the following standing subcommittees: Case Review, Training, and Policy. There is an overlapping membership. Feedback is organized by the secretariat, which administratively services all of the subgroups and the ACPC itself. Feedback to constituent agencies is unclear. One of the posts funded by the ACPC is an inter-agency trainer. The specialist team that services the ACPC is multi-disciplinary.

Like Authority A, decision making is by consensus and there is no conflict-resolution mechanism. The nomination from the ACPC to the Department of Health Programme was for a member of the specialist team to attend the programme. Unlike Authority A, the trainee *was* a member of the ACPC and occupied a strategic position within the organization in relation to child protection.

Possible hypotheses

(a) There are clear lines of authority within agencies and between agencies.

(b)   There is a commitment to multi-disciplinary working and recognition of role differences.

(c)   The organization may be overly dependent on "reticulists" or key individuals who instigate and sustain co-ordination (Hallett & Birchall, 1992).

(d)   Conflict between agencies will be resolved by the specialist team that services the ACPC. However, if the agency and/or discipline is not represented on the specialist team, conflict will continue either by escalating or being avoided, thus producing a splinter group operating outside of ACPC policy, procedures, or general guidance.

This trainee had a clear organizational mandate and occupied a key strategic position within the child protection network. The training strategy developed by the trainee was implemented in the nominating authority and sponsored by the ACPC. Within a month of completion it was written up as a report for the ACPC detailing topics covered, overheads, and articles referred to as well as feedback from course participants.

The role differentiation between disciplines seemed very clear. The trainee was able to increase role differences within her discipline and agency as opposed to across disciplines and by different agencies by clarifying line-management issues in relation to her own post and those of a key group of child protection specialists.

Interestingly, the Development Group failed to work effectively, and at final follow-up the trainee met with the Course Lecturer and Line Manager. The Development Group was seen by the ACPC as redundant, given the structure of the specialist team. The specialist team was an organizational structure that facilitated, enhanced, and modelled multi-disciplinary cooperation in child protection. The degree to which the team worked because of the individuals within it (the reticulist model) or because of the organizational structure is difficult to disentangle. Most probably it was a serendipitous combination. However, the key importance of the team in the smooth running of the ACPC and child protection services is undeniable. Consequently, appointments to these strategic posts would be extremely significant. The specialist team plus co-opted members may have been most appropriate as a Development Group.

A major area of conflict with one of the constituent agencies involved in treatment provision remained problematic throughout participation in the programme. New posts for the specialist team were created to help with the necessary liaison between treatment agencies and to attempt to encompass a wider spectrum of expertise in the specialist team itself.

This ACPC effectively used the Department of Health Programme to increase expertise and to clarify roles and tasks for a key group of professionals. The structure of the ACPC lent itself to the dissemination of information via the "reticulists" in the specialist team. Individuals or agencies within the network of child protection who did not support the "reticulists" would have to find indirect ways of avoiding their sphere of influence.

More detailed consultation with the specialist team about strategies for dealing with recalcitrant and reluctant participants could have been devised. The Development Group could have been a forum for precisely this type of consultation, yet perhaps its novel constitution was perceived as a negative influence on the balance between the ACPC, the specialist team, and child protection services.

Both of these examples describe specific ACPC structures. However, the general patterns have been seen in other ACPCs, often from very different geographical areas. These examples were selected for their similarities in relation to who was seen at final follow-up and the effectiveness (or lack of it) of their Development Groups, and for the striking differences in the structures of their ACPCs. So whilst they may have manifested similarities in some of the outward "behaviour", such as who was present at final follow-up, the different organizational structures within which child protection took place suggest very different reasons for similar "behaviour". The different organizational styles were evident throughout the whole of the Department of Health Programme. The third example illustrates that despite constituting what seems to be an ideal Development Group, correct membership alone does not guarantee an effectively functioning system.

Example 3

In Local Authority C, the Development Group was constituted at the beginning of the training programme by the trainee, her Line Manager, and the chair of the ACPC. In this case the chairperson of the ACPC was a temporary appointment pending radical changes to the ACPC following a serious incident of child abuse. The chairperson of the ACPC came from a voluntary organization rather than Social Services and was involved in a number of other ACPCs. The Development Group consisted of the trainee; her Line Manager, who had a training remit; a Child Protection Co-ordinator, who sat on the ACPC; a Child Psychiatrist, who sat on the ACPC and represented ACPCs on the Programme's Steering Group; a paediatrician, who sat on the ACPC; a Social Services Children's Services Manager, who sat on the ACPC; a Probation Service Manager; who chaired the Development Group; and two practitioners, one from the local authority and one from a voluntary organization, both of whom specialized in direct work with child sexual abuse cases and were delegated to attend by their Line Managers. The group met regularly throughout the two years of the programme.

A training strategy was devised for the five training days. This included a one-day workshop for the Development Group itself, focusing on stress in child protection work; it was to take place on the final training day and was due to occur shortly before the final follow-up with the Course Lecturer and the Social Services Inspectorate.

On the scheduled day a conflict of interests emerged in that the ACPC had a meeting scheduled for the afternoon. Given that the size of the training group was ten, this meant that four members would be leaving half-way through the workshop. The Training Officer who had booked the day was not a member of the ACPC. Yet despite four individuals who were, the clash of dates did not emerge until the morning of the workshop. Additionally, two of the ACPC members were unaware of the afternoon meeting, one of whom had something else booked as well (thus being triple-booked for the afternoon). This put the topic of stress in child protection work into sharp focus. However, it also highlighted an organizational style in which, despite attendance as representatives, *individuals* attended who abdicated their professional responsibility to provide the overview of services or wider perspective that their role gave them and was the reason for their being invited to become members of the Development Group in the first place.

Whilst a training subgroup of the ACPC may have helped prevent such a conflictual situation, the problem of communication between systems seemed to be more fundamental. Given the original support from the ACPC by its then temporary chairperson, who was not a member of the subsequently formed Development Group, one might hypothesize about the handing-over to the new chairperson and the newly constituted ACPC's understanding regarding the commitment required to make best use of its successful nomination onto the programme.

Significantly, in this authority the issue of role confusion was cited as a major contributor in the serious episode of child abuse. In the example above, busy individuals were attending various meetings all about child protection, but they clearly attended as individuals offering those meetings their individual professional overview or special expertise, rather than providing an overview of services or a meta-perspective.

Whilst the goal of the Development Group was clearly laid out, the roles of members remained unclear, despite clarification being offered by the programme during consultations and workshops. The organizational style at higher levels and reflected in the ACPC was one of committed individuals. This led to an inability to spot a time-tabling conflict where training offered to a Development Group and mandated by the ACPC is undermined by the very same ACPC, which arranged a meeting on the same day. This also led to a dilemma for the four participants who had the double commitment—how should they prioritize their commitments? To whom was their loyalty greatest—the Development Group, or the ACPC? Additionally, the ACPC is giving a double message regarding its support for the programme.

Given that this occurred towards the end of the training programme, to what extent had the programme promoted organizational change?

(a)   It highlighted and emphasized the feedback the organization received from an official enquiry.

(b)   It alerted the training representative to the need for better communication between the Training Department and the ACPC.

(c)   It provided individual members of the group with more information about a variety of aspects of sexual abuse.

(d)   It demonstrated the lack of direction from the top of the organization (a feeling confirmed by the practitioners) as well as some of the conflicting messages the organization was giving by posing workers with impossible tasks like being in two places at once.

(e)   It demonstrated that initiatives were more often implemented by middle managers and practitioners. Indeed, the course was one such initiative. Consequently, the biggest impact was felt at the level of middle managers and practitioners where attendance at their allocated training days was high—90% of the target group attended—whereas at higher levels in the organization it was considerably lower, at 50%.

These three examples illustrate the patterns of organizational style reverberating both positively and negatively through the child protection network in any one authority. This is applying systemic ideas to the macro level or organizational context. Through the Department of Health Programme, the importance of the wider organizational context was continually emphasized and brought home as enthusiastic, committed, and skilled trainees attempted to implement training and treatment initiatives in supposedly receptive authorities with little or no success. As they began to attend to organizational variables or to implement their skills more strategically, their success rate increased.

The following chapters amplify and elaborate systemic perspectives in training by looking at the micro level of the course itself, through selection of the course, the trainers, the process of engaging a target audience, and the design of training exercises that enhance a learning system's capacity to learn from itself.

CHAPTER FOUR

If the shoe fits, wear it:
trainers redefined

This chapter examines the selection both of trainers and of courses, which is often delegated to a single individual. Consequently, the choice will reflect many of these individuals' own personal preferences and biases. If a training subgroup were functioning effectively, agencies could pool their knowledge about trainers, courses, and materials.

A large number of training materials have been produced for use in child protection work. *What's in the Box* (Armstrong & Hollows, 1989a) attempts to evaluate them and to make suggestions as to how they might be used. Writing or devising a training pack is extremely difficult because it is easy to minimize the specific and often vital role of the trainers themselves. Many programmes, workshops, packs, etc. work because of the individual skills of a particular trainer.

Consequently, the choice itself—whether to select a trainer to run a workshop, to buy a training pack, or to send someone on a course—will impact on the positive transfer of learning to the work context.

The Child Abuse Training Unit (CATU) has evolved a check-list to be used when evaluating training materials that could usefully be employed when selecting a trainer or course. The check list covers:

(a)   aims;

(b)   content;

(c)   design;

(e)   target group;

(e)   theoretical perspective, values, and philosophy.

These issues are assessed before moving on to look at specific issues in using the training material.

Such a systematic approach by CATU to evaluating training materials demonstrated that non-specific trainer variables probably account for a substantial amount of success in any one package. The selection of a trainer is, then, an especially important task and could usefully be approached in a rigorous fashion vis-à-vis the theoretical perspective, values, and philosophy of the trainer in relation to the training content and aims for a particular target group.

Requests for training in child protection come in many different forms and from many different sources. Equally, trainers come from many disciplines and work in a variety of contexts. Not only do trainers work in different contexts, they also have different labels. For example, what is the difference between a trainer, a lecturer, a teacher, an instructor, a facilitator? Each of these different words, whilst similar, also conveys differences in approach to the task of promoting knowledge and skills.

The verb "to train" perhaps offers the widest range of interpretations and provides trainers with an opportunity to reflect metaphorically on the product of their labours. To train may mean to draw or pull along after one, but can equally denote to hang down so as to drag and trail (*Oxford English Dictionary*). This lassitude in definition is matched by the wide variety of settings in which trainers exist and operate within child protection.

My experiences of being a trainer fall into roughly two categories: (1) that of a trainer who is contracted in by an agency to offer training to a group that has been selected for me and (2) as a trainer who organizes and co-ordinates a training programme where selection of the trainees is by application to the programme (described in chapter two).

THE TRAINING CONTEXT
WITHIN AN ORGANIZATION

In the field of child protection there are professionals who are employed as trainers within departments, usually Social Services. Some ACPCs also employ trainers whose remit is to provide multi-disciplinary training to staff from the constituent agencies involved in the task of child protection. Within my own discipline, clinical psychology, it is rare for there to be someone employed with the sole purpose of training already qualified members of the same discipline. The extent to which training is incorporated into one's own organization is an indication of two paradoxical messages. On the one hand, it reflects the importance of staff development and the need for a continual updating and reflection process on professional issues; on the other, it can imply a lack of confidence inspired by one's core discipline training.

Inadvertently, having a training department can convey a basic dissatisfaction with the qualification training of the workers employed. For many years I have reflected on the irony that the profession that requires the minimum years to qualification (i.e. CQSW) often works with the most complex cases in child protection, whereas those with the maximum number of years to qualification (psychiatry) often work with the most amenable cases in child protection. Additionally, a work context that allows one to select the population one works with is stacked in favour of those with the most number of years of professional training.

Hallett and Birchall (1992) go so far as to state that "pivotal child protection workers [social workers] are severely disadvantaged in dialogue with other members of the interagency system with longer trainings". Couple this with the complex interplay of race, gender, class, and personal experience in forming a professional identity and accessing the training of your choice, and the difficulties of competing agendas in multi-disciplinary training begin to take shape. They often reflect issues that are as yet unresolved at the highest levels of organization.

Training as the solution to such huge social and political problems mirrored in the microcosm of child protection work is both naive and politically convenient. Training is something tangible and measurable. X number of employees received x amount of training. Value for money in training can be reduced to this type of equation. The assumption that training will positively impact on a professional's practice can remain conveniently untested.

Within child protection, perhaps not sufficient attention is paid to other training forums that will increase workers' knowledge, skills, and confidence in doing the work. Whilst training will address some of these issues, there are other effective ways of increasing competencies, not least of which is on-going professional supervision at work.

Over the years the balance between my clinical work and my training work has shifted. Initially the balance was predominantly clinical, whereas latterly it has shifted to training. I am committed to a model in which practice and theory inform each other. This means I try to put my theory into practice, but equally I attempt the reverse, putting practice into theory. I endorse a model of trainer/practitioner because this is a useful link or bridging position. It is important that trainers have some understanding of the reality of doing the work, the context in which it is carried out, and the stresses it generates. Of equal importance, training helps me to reflect on my work. It pushes me to clarify my thinking and to attempt to articulate to others what I think I am doing, in much the same way as writing does.

I have had the experience of being an in-house trainer, by which I mean running training programmes for colleagues employed by the same authority. In common with many in-house trainers, I found that I was valued more when I was contracted out. I suspect that there is a hierarchy regarding which courses to attend. In-house courses—which, paradoxically, may be the most useful in that they will be more in touch with local issues, policies, procedures, and resources—seem to be valued least. Outside courses run at prestigious institutions are often valued most. Somewhere in the middle fall those courses where an outsider is brought in for a local group. In an era of financial constraints, restraints, and value for money, in-house training may come to be seen as an extremely valuable resource, whilst external courses will be seen as too expensive for an organization to support. So the perceived value of courses can be influenced by changes in the wider context.

HYPOTHESES GENERATED
FROM SPECIFIC REQUESTS TO DO TRAINING

In going into an agency as a trainer, one has little control over selection of applicants. This will impact most potently when the trainer attempts to engage the group in the learning task. You may be given information on what previous experience and/or training the participants will have had. Attendance at the course by participants will be dictated by agency expectations. This includes absenteeism, punctuality, and complete attendance of the full course. As an outsider trainer you have no authority to give permission for people not to attend. Unless a training representative is present, I am rarely asked for feedback regarding the group's actual attendance, punctuality, and participation. As an outsider you also do not possess knowledge about local issues that may impinge on the training you are running. This can include previous courses that were very successful or unsuccessful; inter-professional rivalries or conflicts that may be played out in the training course; and professional dissatisfaction with local services, which may include management and supervision.

Good Enough Training: Managing and Developing Training in Child Sexual Abuse (Hollows, Stanton-Rogers, & Armstrong, 1989) attempts to identify some of the issues that will need to be addressed if training opportunities are to be maximized. At an early stage a trainer needs to understand what is termed the climate of training, or the training environment you are going to enter. As an outside trainer it is useful to ask for information regarding the context in which your training will occur. However, you have less control over establishing the wider organizational training ethos.

Items for consideration include:

(a)   selection and course membership;

(b)   evaluation both from participants and from trainer;

(c)   pre-course preparation;

(d)   post-course follow-up.

In offering courses as a contracted-in trainer I have rarely adequately addressed these concerns. With regard to membership, I have frequently inquired as to the gender balance in the training group as well as the ethnic mix. This has sprung out of my experience that a solitary male on a course about sexual abuse frequently made both that individual and the other participants feel uncomfortable. When similar requests were made regarding the ethnic composition of the group, rather different responses were evoked. Monitoring for gender was relatively simple, monitoring for ethnicity more difficult, as it often required a specific question to be included on the application form.

Selection of trainees is almost a misnomer. In my experience the vast majority of trainees arrive on courses because they have applied as opposed to being selected. As an outside trainer, I am not selecting the training group that my course will be given to or my training will be run for. I will be negotiating the training contract with someone who represents either a single constituent agency or a number of agencies engaged in the child protection task. The course will be designed according to what they think are the needs of the course participants. The trainer is selected and matched to a training group the members of which are also selected frequently by the same person or persons, who may or may not be present when the course is running. Consequently the fit between trainer and trainees is based on someone else's perception of both, with little direct negotiation between the two parties. For a one-off training event, this is like a blind date. For a longer training commitment, it is an arranged marriage. The success of either venture is significantly more dependent on the relationship between the two parties than on the organizational context that has brought the two of them together. The likelihood of them uniting against the wider system is greater, and the possibility of promoting positive transfer of learning reduced, as a consequence of this disconnection between the course and the wider, local child-protection systems.

When invited to put on a training course, the invitation often conveys more than a request for specialist input. For example:

*"X.L., course organizer for A.B.C. course, has asked
me to invite you to present the feminist
perspective/issues to the course membership. . . ."*

If the invitation is viewed as a communication about the course as a system and about the organization that is sponsoring it, I believe it communicates some important messages to me as a trainer, should I take up the request. Firstly, the course organizer has asked someone else to approach me. As this is a formal request, why didn't it come from the course organizer? Secondly, there is an apparent inability on the part of the agency sponsoring the course to provide an in-house trainer to present what is termed here as "the feminist perspective". This suggests something about the ethos of the sponsoring agency regarding feminism. It is unlikely in such a large agency that not a single member of staff was either familiar with or identified as a feminist. Thirdly, it seems that the course membership were communicating something to their course organizers regarding the content of the course they were being offered. The request for the feminist perspective input had come from the course membership. This indicates that no participant felt sufficiently empowered to offer to do it for the rest of the course membership. Again it is unlikely that on a whole course no one knew anything about feminist issues in child protection. Additionally, the feminist perspective was not already on the course in a form that satisfied either the members or the course organizer. The solution of the dilemma of wanting to discuss feminism and child sexual abuse but not being able to themselves was to request an outsider to come and facilitate it.

Another example of a similar issue also regarding feminism was a request to do a session on gender, race, and power issues in supervision with a panel of three other presenters, all male, each of whom was doing a major model of change—psychodynamic, behavioural, and systemic—in relation to supervision. The workshop was set up to discuss models of supervision. The framework itself conveys clear messages that the major models of change do not have comments to make about gender and race and that the only way to represent them is to request someone specifically to address them.

Both of the above examples carry paradoxical messages regarding the content of the trainer's material. On the one hand, it is very important and needs to be addressed; on the other, no one else who is presenting can address it. Inadvertently, this approach often marginalizes the very perspective it hopes to introduce.

Sometimes requests for outside trainers spring from a desire to offer an experience of difference for the trainees (Example 1 in chapter three could fall into this category). In these circumstances the training may occur over a longer period, and many different trainers will be invited to present their ideas to the course. It is helpful to have information regarding what previous relevant training participants have had; if the material you present is too novel or dissonant with what has gone before, it is unlikely to facilitate new learning.

Requests can also be received for help regarding the best way to address a particular issue. Also, trainers can be given a brief that is too large to cover in the time allotted. This can be difficult to assess. If a particular group has worked together for some time, they may be able to get through more material in less time because they have more experience of working together as a learning system. In cases such as this, the trainer needs to be clear what can be accomplished in the time available under ideal learning conditions.

No doubt all trainers tire of the comments regarding structural aspects of the training, such as the venue, the food, the acoustics, and so forth. Tedious as these issues may seem, the physical space in which the training occurs and the services that support the training all communicate about the way training is viewed by the organization that is sponsoring it. Indeed, if some of the structural features are dreadful enough, they can impede learning.

An outside trainer is entirely dependent on the internal organizer to arrange these aspects of the training context. On the whole, I am rarely left to wonder where it is I should be and what is the best way to get there. Generally, the room is set up, which conveys an expectancy and a welcome. However, there are occasions when I arrive and find that I am expected to put the chairs out, position the screen, set up the overhead projector, and so on. I am never sure what this is meant to convey to me—a total confidence in my ability to rise to the occasion and be self-sufficient; a comment on my status (not important enough to roll the carpet out yet); or a general approach where everyone is expected to muck in and help make the context more amenable. I will not possess the necessary overview of training in that organization to know if my reception varies from that of any other trainers, or to see if the welcome is gender-mediated, with male trainers being catered for differently than female trainers. Food is frequently laid on, as are tea and coffee. Indeed, some of the supporting services are so good that they become the criteria as to whether or not individuals and trainers continue to apply to do the training.

MAKING THE MOST
OF FEEDBACK IN TRAINING

Evaluation is often an integral part of the course. However, I rarely devise my own evaluation form. Often the agency that has asked me to train uses a standard form for evaluating courses. The completed forms are collated. I have not been informed whether they are reported back to the whole of the course membership. I rarely receive summaries of the evaluation myself. This means that the full benefit of feedback is not being used. The trainees can make comments without having to take on board their own contribution to the establishment of a learning environment.

Trainers are not usually asked for comments regarding the course—such as, if they have run the workshop previously how did this one compare? The opportunity for feedback from the trainer is lost. Management can opt out of the issues arising that specifically concern them and their role in facilitating service delivery. Evaluation needs to be reframed as a feedback task. It needs to be built into the overall design of the course and aim to link to the organizational structures that oversee training such as the training department or the ACPC training subgroup. An example of a course where the feedback component was built in was described in *Social Work Today* by Sarah Borthwick (1991). On this Assessment and Treatment course, the final afternoon was reserved for a meeting between participants and their managers to present management issues that had arisen over the eight weeks the course had run.

A disconnection from the wider system within which child protection takes place can occur when the mechanisms employed for monitoring and evaluating the course are not sufficiently connected onto the organizational structure that commissioned the training in the first instance. The feedback loop between trainer and trainees is an integral part of any training. A trainer solicits it throughout by requesting comments and discussion and through the training exercises that are devised. However, the feedback to the organizational representative is less clearly defined. For example, I have never been asked if any difficulties manifested themselves on the course, or whether I felt particular trainees were capable of doing certain tasks or had achieved a level of skills development that was adequate.

I may do a lot of training, but whether it accomplishes what I think it does is open for discussion. I have no measures by which to assess successful completion of the courses or workshops that I run. Is being invited to contribute regularly a sign of success or of failure?

The absence of formal feedback into the agency that has commissioned the training increases the separation of the training experience from the wider organizational context in which protection work and the new learning is meant to be practised.

Buying-in trainers affords the organization the greatest amount of control in terms both of participants and of the selection of trainers. Buying training packs also provides an agency with a high degree of control. Sending individuals out to attend courses seems to prompt a total abdication of organizational issues other than those regarding time off, fees, and replacement time.

Curry, Caplan, and Knupple (1991) have devised a strategy to help facilitate positive transfer of learning by identifying key players within the workers' network. The Department of Health Postgraduate Training Programme attempts to resolve some of the dilemmas about positive transfer of training skills into the working environment by the use of Development Groups.

The time out from an agency can facilitate learning, but many trainees express dissatisfaction with not being able to put their new learning into practice once they return. If a course runs for a portion of the work week, there is the tension between being a trainee on two days of the week and a fully qualified practitioner the other three days that may make functioning effectively in either role more difficult.

Clearly there is a need to engage managers in the task of selecting candidates for courses. To do so effectively requires the managers to have knowledge regarding their employees and their training needs, the agency training needs and overall training strategy, as well as the various courses being offered—in other words, a complex fit of potentially competing or contradicting needs.

This should encourage training programmes to give clear information regarding the content of the course, its aims, and its learning objectives. This should be coupled with attempts to evaluate the degree to which the course succeeds in achieving its aims. Additionally, it should encourage management to shape the training needs of individuals within the organization to fit with the overall agreed policy and service strategy in child protection.

The feedback into the organization is vital, but confusion arises if the connection between the course and a trainee's employer is not clearly defined at the outset.

In selecting a trainer, an individual trainee may choose a course where the trainer and the models or methods employed will fit with the trainees. When management selects trainees and matches them with courses/trainers, it requires management to have a knowledge of both and of the overall ethos in the organization. Will this course fit with the overall organizational strategy? Consequently, the needs of an individual for professional growth and development may be incompatible with the needs of the organization. Many trainees use outside courses as a springboard for job changes. The partial disengagement from the wider system of work facilitates the total disengagement from the work system.

QUESTIONS TO CONSIDER
REGARDING THE CONTEXT OF TRAINING

As a trainer who thinks systemically, the context in which training is carried out is extremely important.

(a) To what degree is the trainer outside of the system being trained?

(b) Who has requested the training and for what purpose?

(c) How will the course be evaluated? By whom?

(d) What is the feedback mechanism between course participants and trainer?

(e) What is the feedback mechanism between course participants and management?

(f)   What is the feedback mechanism between trainer and management?

(g)   What is the trainer being requested to do?

(h)   Does the request need to be shaped up? Explored in more detail?

(i)   How will that be done? With the person requesting the training on behalf of the organization? Or with the eventual course participants?

(j)   What hypothesis can be generated about why this training is being requested at this time?

(k)   How would the training be modified in light of the hypotheses generated?

CHAPTER FIVE

Engage brain
before disengaging mouth:
are you curious?

E ngagement is a systemic concept that usually refers to the joining process between the therapist and the family. John Burnham (1986) highlights the paucity of literature on the successful convening of families. Additionally, he comments on the role that prestige or status may play in the engaging process. He cites Napier and Whittaker (1978) as describing engagement as the "battle for structure". I have heard Minuchin use the metaphor of dancing to describe not only the process of engagement but also of systemic change. He described watching the family's dance, joining in, and then changing the step. Reflecting back on this metaphor, he did not at that time mention "taking the lead" to change the step or that as a man it may be easier to take the "lead" given society's expectations that men lead and women follow.

Engagement is an interactive process with the intention of forming a new context within which information can be explored, developed, applied, connected, or rejected in relation to other experiences we have within other contexts. In this chapter, engagement will be used to describe the process of joining with participants of a training event.

In earlier chapters, I have outlined some of the organizational factors that impact on any training experience. The extent to which any individual trainer has to engage a particular group in the learning process will be dependent on the wider context within which the training has been placed.

A one-off lecture to a group of people convened for a larger conference may seem like a simple engagement task. The audience is usually captive, and unless you have the misfortune of getting the afternoon slot when everyone's blood is rushing to their stomachs, as opposed to their brains, your contribution can be delivered with little warm-up and negotiation. This learning context is a good way of imparting information to a large number of people simultaneously. It is also a good example of a monological perspective (Goolishian & Winderman, 1988).

Frequently, as an invited speaker you are presenting in the one-up position in relation to an audience. The situation Virginia Goldner (1991) describes of an empowered, sophisticated group of listeners should remind presenters of the precarious position they are in if they assume that expertise rests only with themselves. However, it often is the presenter's status that engages the audience. In the same article, Virginia Goldner comments on this by referring to "'star' presenters who often don't bother to prepare (their presence is supposed to be enough . . .)".

How does this affect an individual's capacity to learn? If people hold beliefs about who they can learn from and this relates to the status of the individual doing the teaching, then clearly learning will take place because it is connected to the individual's belief system about how one learns. To choose such a context to learn new material indicates a belief that this is considered possible by the individual participants, whether they be "cowed or combative" by the context (Goldner, 1991).

Beliefs about how one learns are especially important when training is with a multi-disciplinary audience. Different disciplines may hold different and incompatible beliefs about how learning takes place (Charles & Stevenson, 1990). Thrown together into a joint training venture, such epistemological differences regarding learning are sure to arise. This is not to say that all members from the same discipline have similar training experiences, but qualifying to be an 'x' may act as a significant context marker when in a multi-disciplinary form.

Gender, race, and status will also impact on the beliefs people have about learning. For example, new information or learning about sexual abuse did not reach certain professional circles until the information was imparted by someone perceived as having status within those professional circles. Learning is frequently seen as a linear phenomenon where someone older, wiser, and generally of high status imparts knowledge to someone younger, less wise, and, by inference, of lower status. It is not surprising then that sexual abuse was taken more seriously as an issue when male professionals started to raise issues that feminists and females had raised earlier.

As a feminist and a systemic thinker, I can understand why a message is received by a wider audience when the messenger is changed. It may be seen as a more effective way of engaging a particular target audience to refer to a higher-order context, that the message is more important than the messenger.

Engagement is affected by the gender and race not only of the presenter, but also of the participants and the interaction between them. Whether a particular audience will engage with you depends on the context marker they prioritize. It may be the venue that has drawn them; or the organization that organized the event; or the speakers, either the range invited or specific individuals. What is subsequently actually said and how it is said will be secondary.

Specific strategies for engaging the participants in learning about what you have to say may have to be devised. For example, many years ago the London Rape Counselling and Research Project was asked to do a presentation at the Annual Police Surgeons' Conference. As a then current member of the collective, I agreed to do it. I presented a paper entitled "Rape and Forensic Practice" (Smith, 1979), which I read out loud to a huge audience of virtually all white male police surgeons. The paper was based on the work of the Rape Crisis Centre and made very clear critical comments concerning current forensic practice, criticisms that had been made by the consumers of the service—women who had been raped and had reported this to the police.

The centre had researched the task well, providing me with copies of appropriate articles from the police surgeons' professional journals. I used material from these articles in my talk—an example of learning to use the idiosyncratic language of the group you are hoping to engage. Indeed, I invoked a well-known forensic aphorism known as Locard's principle ("Every contact leaves a trace") in a metaphorical sense, enjoining the audience to think of contact in a more human/humane way.

The impact of the talk was palpable in part because the criticism was so unexpected, but also because it was based not only on women's experience of forensic services, but also on published material from the profession's own journals.

One article on forensic medical examinations referred to women as "pussies" (Paul, 1977). This article was used as evidence that sexism and a gross lack of sensitivity to all women, but especially to women who had been raped, was flourishing within their professional ranks. Whilst the author of this paper was not present at the conference, the article had been published and would have been passed by an editorial group, who were present. Additionally, there had been no outcry in the subsequent journals regarding the offensive material. Consequently, the audience had to accept some responsibility for the views and to recognize the consequences of such views being published. It confirmed women's feelings that they were not being treated with sensitivity and respect.

Later, at another conference, I shared a platform with the aforementioned author and heard his "pussy talk" first-hand. The plenary was predictably explosive as an unsuspecting chairperson was confronted with an irrepressible force meeting an unmoveable object. I cannot say I handled this interaction with strategic integrity. However, this experience taught me to enquire about other speakers at conferences and on panels, which would enable me to make an informed decision regarding my participation and presentation and to plan how I might handle differences should they emerge.

With large audiences, you know less about them individually. You will have to decide what aspects of yourself or your work you wish to share. Feedback about the fit between what you have prepared and what they have come for is most often non-verbal.

People leaving, lots of shuffling, coughing, sleeping, are all signs that engagement has occurred at a different level than the one intended! Who comes up to talk with you later also gives you some feedback regarding how successfully you have engaged individuals. When black participants engage me as a white presenter in more detailed discussion of my material, I take this as feedback that I have conveyed an understanding and willingness to address issues that are a primary concern to them. Additionally, it shows a willingness to enter into a dialogical perspective (Goolishian & Winderman, 1988), on both our parts. Who feels able to approach a presenter after a presentation is affected by a range of variables in the same way as who feels able to ask questions or make comments at large events. Sometimes you can be surprised.

At a 3-day training event that I ran with a colleague, one participant arrived each day and promptly feel asleep in the front row, waking for tea, coffee, lunch, and the end of each day. On the last day, she woke as usual at the end, but before leaving came up to the teaching team to thank us for the workshop, saying "You have really opened my eyes!" We all smiled and nodded, marvelling at the metaphor she chose to describe her learning experience over the last three days.

Engagement must be thought of in relation to the parameters of the training experience. Arriving for a specific and limited input requires a different strategy than conducting a one-day workshop or a course that runs throughout an academic year.

In defining who you are, your approach to the work, your philosophy or value base, you are setting the frame within which learning with you may take place. This frames learning as an interactive phenomenon in which the parameters are multi-dimensional and interact on many levels simultaneously. Equally, learning may take place outside the context set aside for it.

SYSTEMIC COMMENTS
ON WARM-UP EXERCISES

The use of warm-up exercises to facilitate the engagement process is frequently recommended. This is an example of applying techniques from successful group work to the training context.

However, careful thought needs to go into the selection of a warm-up exercise. What messages are you conveying to the group about the learning context? Equally important, not all warm-up exercises decrease anxiety. Some, paradoxically, increase anxiety.

Using experiential techniques taken from a therapeutic context into the training arena can blur the boundaries between professional training and personal therapy. Additionally, it confuses the meaning of the term experiential. In adult learning, an experiential approach refers to the recognition of individual's previous life/work experiences and building on them. Many times in training it seems to be used to describe a process whereby an individual experiences something on the training course itself. The guided fantasy exercise described in the Bexley Joint Investigation Training Programme (Metropolitan Police & Bexley Social Services, 1987) is an example of this. In this exercise participants are relaxed and then guided back to childhood and encouraged to imagine a sexually abusive episode to sensitize them to the issues their child clients might have. This imaginal experience of sexual abuse is supposed to produce insight in course participants. Whilst extreme, it demonstrates an "experiental" approach.

In multi-disciplinary training, it may be tempting to use warm-up exercises that engage people on a personal level as a way of avoiding conflict that would arise if participants were engaged at the professional level immediately. Engaging participants as people is a way of using the "lowest common denominator" approach. However, this approach fails to recognize that context markers are perhaps infinite, as people can be divided into males and females, white people and black people, and so forth; so choosing the people level of engagement may mean you avoid conflict at one level, only to have it emerge at another. Consequently, expecting and welcoming conflict as the expression of difference and providing a context in which difference is the springboard for the dialectic is perhaps a better way of engaging.

Additionally, deprofessionalizing people involved in child protection work is perhaps not the best way to enhance job performance in relation to specific tasks.

USING PROFESSIONAL CONTEXT MARKERS
IN ENGAGEMENT

A workshop at the Excellence in Training Conference 1991, held by Dale Curry and Peggy Caplan, introduced the notion that, in all training groups, participants could be classed as learners, vacationers, or prisoners. The challenge for any trainer is to convert the prisoners and the vacationers to learners, or, failing that, to minimize the potentially negative consequences their presence might have on the group task of learning.

It can be helpful for a trainer to be able to identify who has come to the event most ready to learn and who may need additional help. Brief introductions concentrating on where someone works reinforces the professional context. It is important that everyone introduces themselves and says where they work. As an outside speaker it is a concrete way in which you engage or join with each member who has attended, but it also gives you information about the structure of the system that will be engaged in the learning task. For example, do people who work in the same place all sit together? Which places are represented? Are there significant ones missing? This may be hard to assess if you are an outside trainer. However, you can ask the group if anyone or any place is missing that they would have expected to be present. This underlines the trainer's dependence on the training group for information regarding local issues and helps to foster an atmosphere of mutual dependence.

If, after introductions on a joint investigation course with police and Social Services, you were greeted with the seating arrangements shown in Figure 2, what hypothesis might you generate about joint investigation? About the training course? The seats were arranged in four rows, lecture style; participants picked their own seats.

Asking how people heard about the course or got onto it is useful since it gives you information regarding the organizations they have come from. This can sometimes identify "prisoners"—i.e. explicit "I was sent" messages.

Getting people to reflect on what they would like to learn can help a trainer locate their contribution to that process. This also provides an opportunity to renegotiate the training contract between the participants and the trainer. It will identify whether there

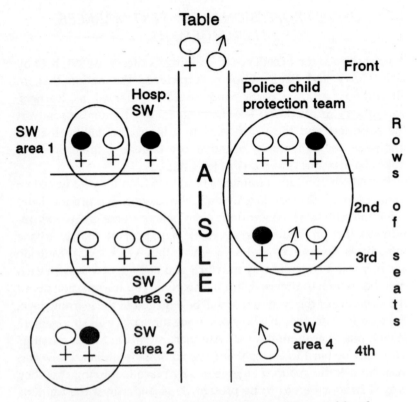

Participants encircled worked together daily outside of
the course. Shaded figures represent minority ethnic
professionals

Figure 2:   Seating arrangement

is a consensus about the content and aims of the training, or a
divergence. This may give the trainer additional information about
the organization that arranged for the training to take place and
how the organization then conveyed the information to the potential consumers of the training.

Many participants, when asked what they are hoping to learn
from the day, do not know what to say. As the trainer you are
greeted by resounding silence. In part this demonstrates the
newness of the system and individual participants' uncertainty regarding the way this system will function. It also is a reflection of

the passive approach to learning that many of us have experienced through our education. It can be difficult to identify what you do not know and consequently what you would like to know. These represent only a few of the many other hypotheses that could be generated; however, *any* comments indicate curiosity and should be noted. They will help a systemic trainer hypothesize, formulate, and design exercises that will connect any "new" learning to "old" learning. They may also indicate the primary preoccupations of individuals within the group that may impede the learning of the whole group.

SYSTEMIC APPROACHES TO THE TASK
OF ENGAGING A NEW GROUP IN LEARNING

Example 4

The following training initiative was carried out on behalf of a Development Group from the Department of Health Postgraduate Training Programme. The topic "Group Work in Sexual Abuse Cases" was identified as a priority training need. The programme consisted of five training days. It was designed as an introductory-level course to be offered throughout the county. It was intended that the course would identify a core group of practitioners who were committed to running group work and who could form the nucleus of workers to facilitate the creation of a rolling programme of groups for the country as a whole. This would reduce duplication of services. The programme was co-run by myself as an outside trainer and by an internal trainer, both of us white women, with the express intention that the internal trainer would be able to repeat and develop the training initiative. The first day was offered to managers who would nominate practitioners to attend the relevant days of the four-day programme on group work. This was designed to allow for a range of different skills and experience to be catered for. The first day was an introductory workshop on group work as a modality. The following three days concentrated on specific client groups that had been identified by the Development Group; these were children as victims, non-abusing parents and carers, and children as perpetrators. It was expected that some workers might attend two days, possibly the introductory and one other client-focused workshop. The Development Group, with help from Social Services Training Department, took responsibility for administering and circulating details about the course. A large number of places were reserved for a particular division of the county, as the internal trainer came from this division.

The managers' course seemed well attended. Twenty participants arrived representing Health, Social Services (the majority), and the Police. There were no representatives from Education or Probation. This indicates immediately either a communication problem (i.e. they were not informed) or that this topic was not seen as a high priority or relevant to that agency. Additionally, the Training Department that administered the programme had expected forty participants, which meant that 50% did not turn up on the day. This seems to indicate that it was seen as a priority at the time of booking but not at the time the training took place. A more detailed follow-up of the reasons for absence would have to be conducted to generate other more specific hypotheses regarding the high failure rate, although some ideas began to emerge from what was said by those who did attend.

Of those who did come on the day, the majority were unaware of the follow-up workshops for their practitioners. When asked what they hoped to get out of the day, many expressed confusion and revealed uncertainty as to whether they were going to retain their current jobs. It was apparent to the trainers that the timing of this initiative was unhelpful and that the content of the day had been designed for a more stable management group. Additionally, it was clear that the practitioners who were booked into the following workshops would not be connected to these managers. The training day had to be adapted to deal with this information. So rather than assuming that group work was a useful service development, this assumption was explored within the context of the wider organizational changes going on in the Health and Social Services. The managers were asked to discuss where a group work programme might fit into the new organizational structures, who (as in which constituent agency) should carry responsibility for developing this service, and what information would different divisions (in this case purchasers and providers) need regarding group work.

This approach identified a range of issues that needed to be taken forward. The group was able to identify which forum issues needed to be addressed and who should take responsibility for doing so. The workshop also identified a structural difficulty regarding identification of children for treatment following disclosure of sexual abuse. The procedures of this county led to many investigations being conducted by primary investigation teams which then did not go on to be case-conferenced. Many of the police personnel continued to worry about children they had seen who they felt needed treatment regardless of the outcome of the investigation. There was no identified structure for monitoring or referring these children on once they had been through the investigative process. The police managers were able to pass on their workers' concerns to other managerial colleagues who more obviously had a responsibility for providing treatment services.

Engaging these managers in a learning experience, regarding group work for sexually abused children and their families, was extremely difficult. Their collective level of anxiety was high and the organizational uncertainty regarding the future of their jobs and the structure of the department meant that the training initiative, despite its high priority, needed to be scheduled at a time when managers could think more strategically about treatment services in sexual abuse work. This was fed back to the ACPC through the Development Group.

Not surprisingly, the match between practitioners and their managers did not exist. The course participants shared their managers' uncertainties regarding the future direction of their agencies. Rather than individual workers consuming the four days as modules, they attended all four days. Their need for contact with other practitioners was high. The level of expertise ranged from no experience at all, to workers who were extremely experienced in group work for sexually abused children. Their training needs were very disparate. This became obvious when we introduced the course and the thinking behind its design. The rationale for the course had clearly not percolated out to potential participants.

Engaging a group with such disparate training needs at a time when management support is clearly absent requires careful attention. The boundaries around the training group were clearly drawn and emphasized, as the wider context was not providing the necessary stability for the workers to continue either their professional development or the delivery of a treatment service.

The trainers had to adapt material to incorporate the differences within the group. The dilemma was how to engage both experienced and inexperienced workers in thinking about providing a group work programme in the county. Initially, there was little sharing in the group, with some more experienced members coming late and leaving early. The more experienced members remained quiet when larger group discussions happened, but they dominated small group discussions. This required the course trainers to modify their approach to the material. They needed to engage the more experienced members as co-trainers or coaches to the less experienced practitioners. The course trainers needed to present their own development over time, highlighting former incompetencies and new skills learned as a result of experiences and/or new learning. By the end of the four-day course the training group was engaged in the task of learning about group work and discussing what organizational factors made it difficult for a comprehensive group work programme to be implemented in the county. They identified various ways of raising the issue of group work with the relevant managers. A smaller subsystem continued working together after the course, and it was more able to recruit other workers to co-run groups with more experienced workers as a way of sharing and providing on-the-job training.

In the latter example, the trainers had to engage the more "resistant" members of the learning system if the training was to be effective and promote change within and across agencies. It can be tempting to stick to your programme despite evidence to suggest it needs to be modified. It is also easy to overlook "resistant" members of training groups and hope that they will come round. However, my experience indicates that a new training system will take time to devise its own methods of dealing with the "resistant" members. In a one-off workshop, it will fall to the trainer(s) to deal with it. Failure to do so generally impedes learning, not just for one member, but for the whole learning system.

Example 5

The following training workshop was run for experienced team leaders within Social Services in a large county council. The focus was on supervision of child sexual abuse cases. This had been identified as a priority training issue by the Development Group. The aims of the workshop were clearly spelt out in the material sent out by the training department prior to the course being run. These aims were as follows:

(a)   to equip supervisors to perform the complex task of enabling staff to work sensitively, carefully, and confidently with all members of the family and with other professionals in cases of child sexual abuse;

(b)   to enable supervisors to make sound professional judgements in the field of child sexual abuse;

(c)   to develop the ability of the supervisors to build a supportive relationship with the worker, within which anxiety is appropriately contained and highly emotive issues can be discussed openly;

(d)   to enable supervisors to demonstrate confident use of authority and the ability to make considered decisions in the best interests of the child.

Reflecting back, the aims of the workshop were too ambitious for a single day, and they were framed in such a way that they implied that the supervisors were not already doing these things.

The workshop was taught by an outside trainer (myself) and by an internal trainer, both of us white women. Neither of us was a Social Services team leader. When participants introduced themselves, a white male identified himself as a team leader for sixteen years, having worked in the field of sexual abuse before it was fashionable not to do so. None of the other participants voiced such a clear challenge to the trainers. When asked what they were hoping to get out of the training, the very experienced team leader said he would wait and see. He was at least curious! Other participants raised The Children Act 1989 and how this would affect supervision of child sexual abuse cases, and one of them referred to the pre-course material and the workshop contents indicated in the programme.

This introduction clearly showed a misfit between the trainers and the participants. Despite these contraindications for proceeding with our original programme, we committed a basic training error: we gave them the material we and the Development Group thought they should have. Their responses were predictable. They knew everything we presented. Over the lunch break, things polarized. Returning from lunch, all the men sat together behind a table at the back of the room, leaving the women, including both trainers, sitting in a "nice" circle.

Despite the escalation, we proceeded with the afternoon programme, which involved the internal trainer presenting material on the impact of child sexual abuse work on the workers themselves. We should have made more of an attempt to re-engage the distant subgroup by asking if they wished to join the circle or perhaps to explore why they preferred to participate in the workshop by sitting behind a table at the back of the room.

By coffee, the experienced team leader refused to continue to participate. He said he had seen enough and decided he had not learnt anything so far and did not think he would by the end of the programme. A few other participants also decided to leave, including some of the other men. The majority of the participants remained.

The outcome was predictable from the outset. We clearly did not consider how to successfully engage the whole group in the learning task. Gender issues had been highlighted, which perhaps facilitated the polarization along gender lines. Gender messages from two women to a mixed group of men and women are often received as persecutory messages by the men, and sometimes by some of the women. Similarly, race messages given by two black trainers to a mixed audience where white workers are in the minority can also be perceived as persecutory by the white workers. This is an example of where a different messenger might have been useful.

The refusal to participate was expressed following the internal trainer's presentation. We speculated on why this might have happened. We considered my status as an outsider and hypothesized that being the Course Lecturer may have prevented participants from directly confronting me with their dissatisfaction regarding the course, reserving it instead for their colleague who was training with me.

By not engaging the participants, we inadvertently patronized them. Whilst this was clearly not our intent, the effect of our actions became perverted by the context in which they were implemented

(Morin, 1982, quoted in Selvini-Palazolli, 1989). After discussing with the group how best to proceed from this point, we were able to develop a dialogue about the training needs of team leaders—the competing demands on their time to perform both professional supervision and managerial tasks within a Social Services Department undergoing organizational changes, with a major new piece of legislation about to be implemented for which they had not yet received training. In effect, we ended the day where we should have begun.

CHAPTER SIX

Interventions
to the learning system

My any training packs and exercises are published for other trainers to use. Whilst these may contain general comments about the target audience and the general level of experience, very little has been written about whether a particular training group is ready for a particular training exercise. If training exercises or small group tasks are seen as interventions to a learning system, then they can be designed with a specific group in mind or modified to deal with some of the information about the training group obtained during the training itself.

Universal prescriptions in training should be used with caution. For example, the guided fantasy exercise (mentioned previously in chapter five) used in the Bexley Joint Investigation Training Programme requires a high level of trust not only in the trainers but also in the other participants. It has not always been well received and it has also attracted a degree of negative criticism (Kelly & Regan, 1990; Byrne & Patrick 1990). The exercise puts participants in a vulnerable position, not only in relation to the trainers, who do not do the exercise, but also in relation to other participants and possibly their employing authorities. It poses dilemmas for workers about the degree to which they wish to reveal aspects of themselves, is possibly dangerous for those participants where the abuse episode is not a fantasy but a real childhood experience, and could cause potential damage to participants who had not been sexually abused. Given these reservations and risks, it would be unwise to use it as a general exercise with just any audience. Additionally, the effect an experience such as this has on an individual's capacity to learn should be taken into account.

EXPLORING THE BOUNDARIES
OF THE LEARNING SYSTEM

The previous example of guided fantasy is used as an introductory exercise on day 2 of a longer programme. The two days are meant to be a warm-up experience to engage the training group in the task of learning about joint investigation.

In addition to the guided fantasy exercise described above, at the end of the first day of the programme participants were asked to pair off and each in turn to relate their most recent or first sexual experience, with the other person acting as investigator (Metropolitan Police & Bexley Social Services, 1987). The skill and commitment of the trainers to the necessity and importance of these exercises contributed to participants doing them. However, in less experienced or less committed hands, the possibility for disaster is high. That these exercises were done at all, by competent motivated professionals, demonstrates the high level of commitment to delivering a better service.

It also demonstrates how trainers can use the authority vested in them by the organization to get participants to do things they might not otherwise do. It would perhaps be more interesting as a learning point to explore with the group how they might manage to do these exercises, but without actually doing them. What would happen to the learning system if someone overtly refused to do them? Is the experience of doing exercises such as these necessary to become better investigators? This would promote learning about learning. Adapting some of these exercises can produce different and perhaps additional learning outcomes.

For example, just setting up the exercise of sharing your most recent or first sexual experience by getting participants to think about doing it, rather than actually doing it (Georgina Robinson, personal communication), usually leads to an outpouring of anxious feelings at the very thought of having to pair up with someone to do the exercise. This can usefully lead on to considering what would be a safe context in which such intimate material could be explored. Doing the exercise in this way also helps investigators relate personal feelings to their professional practice without having to reveal personal information about themselves. This allows participants to maintain privacy and think about the feelings of the child in investigative work, provides greater choice to individual participants, and effectively deals with the setting of a safe context for work.

It addresses the issues of authority both within the training context and also, more importantly, within the child protection services. Given that these experiential exercises from the Bexley Training Programme occur at the beginning of the course, the power imbalance is tipped in favour of the trainers. They know the contents of the programme. They do not have to participate in the exercises, thus drawing a boundary around their own personal experiences. They have an organizational mandate to do the training programme. The likelihood that an individual member will challenge or refuse is small, and the consequences for an individual of doing so, unknown. This parallels the abuse experiences of the victim.

These exercises have been chosen because they are well known, represent an "experiential approach", are prescribed in joint investigation training from a universal prescription, and have generated specific critical comments, and they raise important organizational issues regarding the content of training programmes.

If, for instance, an individual is sent to a training programme but refuses to do certain parts of the programme, will this jeopardize their future work prospects? If an individual does these exercises and is seriously disturbed by them, will their organization be told? What follow-up will be offered? Will this affect their future job prospects? If they disclose personal information such as experience of sexual abuse in childhood, will this be passed on? What if they disclose abusing behaviour? Will this be passed on? If the training is run by an outside trainer and someone experiences profound disturbance as a consequence of doing experiential exercises, can the trainer be held responsible for negligence? Whose responsibility is it to select course participants for courses with an experiential (as in the Bexley programme) component? If an individual refuses to continue with a course because of exercises they consider unethical or damaging, do they still have the right to complain about the experience?

Very few of these issues have clear answers. They are raised to highlight the issues of using quasi-therapy techniques whilst doing training. In a book on systemic perspectives on training, I want to be clear that thinking systemically about training and training groups is intended not to pathologize individuals or organizations but to encourage trainers to think about process, context, and patterns that impact on the training experience and where possible to design exercises that are syntonic with the wider training aims of facilitating working together to protect children and the responsible exercise of authority.

Exercises or small group tasks can be viewed as interventions to the learning system. They may highlight important preoccupations that might impede learning, may reinforce professional role aspects of the learning task, and should lead to assessment of the functioning of the group as a whole before embarking on new learning.

Warm-up exercises should help both trainer and trainees to explore the boundaries of the learning system. The exercises should also help the trainer to hypothesize about the learning system and adapt material in line with these hypotheses (Boston & Draper, 1985). Using warm-up exercises that involve disclosure of personal material immediately presents individuals with loyalty conflicts and boundary confusion regarding private and professional space. It can also create a direct challenge to the authority of the trainer by uniting the training group against the trainer, by refusing to comply with a set task.

If the group you are training works together a lot and consequently has experience as a system, it can be useful to ask them to identify their usual sabotage techniques. These techniques can then be reframed as an indicator to the trainer that the course needs to be modified in some way to facilitate the full participation of the membership (Boston & Draper, 1985).

For example, a training day was run for a small group of very experienced practitioners who met regularly as a group to discuss issues regarding case work and professional development. I was asked to do some training for them. As a warm-up they were asked to let me know in what way they, as a group, stopped discussions or avoided difficult areas. They generated the following list:

(a)   arriving late;

(b)   not arriving at all;

(c)   preoccupation with lunch;

(d)   people leaving throughout the day—e.g. going to the loo;

(e)   people leaving the group—in a wider context;

(f)   realignment process;

(g)   previous issues from other training, particularly the two-day residential as a group;

(h)   differences in the way that you interpret the job;

(i)   is it a group that always has a missing member?

This exercise helped me as the outside trainer to become more engaged with the learning system. It also drew a boundary around the learning system and marked it out as different to their usual meetings.

EXERCISES DESIGNED
TO PROMOTE WORKING TOGETHER

If one of the aims of training in child protection is to promote an atmosphere of mutual respect and co-operative working together, then the learning system should reflect this ideal in the way it runs and tasks are set. I try to do this by designing exercises where smaller subgroups do a portion of the whole task. This means that the whole group is dependent on each other for the task to be completed. For example, I have used the following exercise to help people discuss building an index of suspicion in child sexual abuse cases.

Using the following age categories, 0–5, 5–12, 12+ years, make a list of signs and symptoms that might indicate that sexual abuse is occurring. Weight the symptoms as follows—red for alert signs or high probability, green for go on with the investigation, or blue to signify cold signs where sexual abuse is one hypothesis amongst many.

Initially, the training group was divided into an arbitrary number of smaller groups and given a time to complete the whole task. The feedback took longest for the first group to report back, dwindling as each group got up and repeated some information, or added something different. After a while it became boring. Additionally, the debates in the small groups often were repeated in the larger groups, especially on items that people could not agree on, thus reproducing more of the same material.

Feedback from participants and from other trainers (Davies, Kidd, & Pringle, 1987) encouraged me to change aspects of the task. First, it was important to stress that none of the signs were indicators in and of themselves or that they proved that sexual abuse had happened. Making a list and weighting the indicators was part of hypothesizing, which could be tested by further investigation. This introduces a necessary role of neutrality into such a highly charged subject. What is the most likely explanation for this type of behaviour? Additionally, *doing* the exercises was more important than what was done—the actual process rather than the content.

In redesigning the exercise, I started to break the task down so that the whole group became dependent on the smaller groups doing a portion of the task. I made three small groups and assigned each a different age category to consider. I asked them to concentrate on the red alert signs first and to be prepared to feed them back to the larger group. I gave examples of red alert signs with benign explanations—thus disqualifying both the example and myself—emphasizing that sexual abuse was only a possible explanation. I asked them to mark items where they, as a small group, could reach a consensus regarding the weighting and those where they disagreed. At the feedback, each group took responsibility for presenting their material. Before this, however, I asked for general comments about doing the exercise. I shared the patterns I had observed over time using the exercise; most groups could generate lists of indicators that were generally similar, but they found them hard to weight, preferring to put everything into the green or blue category and nothing in the red. Asking for general comment on the exercise reinforces the boundary around the whole group and puts their work into the wider context of other professionals also struggling with making judgements regarding the likelihood of sexual abuse occurring.

Each small group presented their lists to the whole group. After each age range I shared my list and talked about the similarities and differences between our lists. I tried to explain why I put things in certain categories. The differences on the whole are small and generally reflect more a hesitancy for people to feel confident about their assessments and to place indicators in the red alert section. However, over time this too has changed as professionals become clearer about what might indicate sexual abuse. Whilst my list becomes seen as the expert list, it also contains comments, reflections, and debates of many individuals who participated in the training programmes I ran using this exercise. Their comments and questions helped focus and clarify some of my descriptions.

The redesigned exercise helps to foster a sense of mutual interdependence rather than set up an atmosphere of competition between groups and possibly between the trainees and the trainer. It also helps to establish what, if any, consensus exists about the indicators of sexual abuse, and it conveys a message that differences can be tolerated. Warm-up exercises and those designed to promote working together should help the learning system establish its consensus domain.

EXERCISES USING DIFFERENCE CREATIVELY

Whilst it is important and necessary to establish a degree of consensus on training courses, to promote new learning some differences will have to be explored. Using difference creatively within the training context is important and sometimes very difficult.

Given the split in the training group described in the previous chapter (Figure 2, chapter five), it was important that any training exercises were designed with this in mind. Breaking the group into pairs and occasionally threesomes, all containing at least one police officer and one Social Services employee, and focusing on the details of planning and conducting an investigation, helped contain the split between the two departments and the fragmentation of the Social Services Department. Establishing the consensus domain was the first prerequisite before exploring the considerable differences between departments—Police and Social Services—and within the department—the different area teams in Social Services. The learning system in this situation was comprised of many subgroups with participants' loyalties primarily to the smaller subgroup rather than the larger learning system. This was reflected not only in the seating arrangements, but also in the informal contexts such as tea breaks and lunch, where on the whole the group fragmented into subgroups.

At a different training event, it was hoped that the issue of gender in relation to the supervision process could be explored. In preparing this event, the theoretical material presented was adapted from material on cross-cultural competence and experience of difference used by Terry Cross (1991). The learning group as a whole found it difficult to express a group view that gender impacted either on the supervision process or on direct clinical work. Given that this is a core assumption of mine, it was necessary to explore this difference. An exercise was designed for participants which was intended to highlight the importance of gender. The exercise involved small groups in generating solutions or strategies to situations that had come up in supervision. One set of small groups had gender-unspecified conditions, whilst the other groups had the same scenarios but with the gender specified. For example: "At the end of a clinical placement during the final supervision session, the trainee, after giving the supervisor a thank-you gift, wanted to hug the supervisor." Here, the genders of the trainee and the supervisor are unspecified, and the small group with this example must discuss roles without knowledge of the gender of the people who occupy the roles. Will this make a difference to the strategies or solutions they generate? Can the small groups generate solutions in the absence of this gender information?

All groups were given the same amount of time to accomplish the task. The groups were unaware that they were operating under different conditions. When the groups came together for feedback, we made some predictions about the nature of the tasks. We thought that the gender-unspecified groups would have needed more time and consequently may not have finished the task, and that the discussions in the gender-specified groups would have focused on different issues. The purpose of the exercise was to highlight the impact of gender on problem solutions. It was made clear that there were no right answers but the assumption was that knowing the gender of the trainee and the supervisor in the scenarios did affect both the speed at which the task could be done and the type of solutions considered. At the end of this training event, the group felt able to express a view that reflected an awareness of gender difference which would enable them to begin to move on to developing new strategies for dealing with it, both within supervision which was the intended focus, but also within clinical work—a serendipitous by-product.

An awareness and acceptance of difference is one of the first steps towards developing cross-cultural competence (Cross, 1991). I have also used similar versions of the exercise but in relation to race, where small groups are given the same scenarios but race is varied. This allows a training group to explore what difference (if any) it would make to their practice if the race of the client was changed. It also helps to highlight what assumptions they make about race when using case material. A very substantial number of training packages use case material but do not specify race, except when mentioning black children. The use of names is often meant to prompt or cue the training group as to the ethnic origin of the client. However, that assumes a cultural knowledge on the part of the training group which they may not possess.

To develop awareness of difference, it is important that difference is unhooked from right-and-wrong approaches to the material. Here the concept of therapeutic neutrality can be used effectively. Whilst engagement might be easier when there are perceived similarities vis-à-vis race and gender of the participants, it may be more difficult to explore differences or to disengage at the end of a piece of work. The reverse may be true when there are differences across race and gender between participants.

Example 6

At one training workshop the learning system was comprised of twelve white women, one white man, and one black woman. During the course, discussion regarding male sexual offenders arose. The single black female participant and the single white male participant reflected on their pairing up within the learning system. Despite differences within the majority white women group (such as class, religion, sexual orientation), the feeling of sameness was overwhelming to the visibly different black woman and white man. The black woman reported feeling conflicted—should she join with the women? However, her empathy with the lone white male was greater, and she joined with him. The course itself was on working with families where sexual abuse has occurred. The feelings of anger and rejection, and the desire to find someone to blame so often generated by this type of work, were present in the learning system. Rather than carry on with the planned exercises, there was a discussion regarding these feelings and the impact they might have on an individual's capacity to learn and do the work. It was at this point that the observations of "the pair" were offered to the group. The inhibiting effect this might have had on group learning was avoided.

Example 7

This final example is taken from a small group at a national conference on training in child protection, sponsored by the Training Advisory Group on Sexually Abused Children. Each small group was asked to design a course in child protection outlining its aims, learning outcomes, specific objectives, limitations, and necessary prerequisites.

The small group I was working with was very diverse, and the whole of the working time could have been taken up by identifying which course to design. The group, however, contained two sub-groups: managers and practitioners. Prior to splitting them into two small groups, the gender balance of the group was about 50:50. However, this split produced clear gender differences, with the majority of men in the managers' group and the majority of women in the practitioners' group. The ethnic balance of the group was non-existent, with a lone black participant. To enhance working together and to promote an understanding of difference, I asked the managers' group to design a course for practitioners, and vice versa.

Structuring the exercise in this way allowed for the diverse experiences, but also offered an opportunity for practitioners and managers to receive feedback in a different context. None of the practitioners was managed by any of the managers. This provided a degree of freedom for both practitioners and managers. They could make comments that would not continue to affect working relationships outside the course. This is important to remember for local training events, where managers and practitioners train together. The boundary around the learning system is more diffuse and comments made in one context have more potency in other, shared contexts.

The practitioners who designed a course for managers responded to the questions of the exercise outlined above as follows:

1. *Aims of course*
   (a) To update management on current issues surrounding child sexual abuse;
   (b) to outline what is special in this area of work;
   (c) to explore management thinking on agency objectives;
   (d) to look at management issues in developing caring and supporting their staff.

2. *Learning outcomes*
   (a) To enable participants to develop a complete understanding of the basic needs and dilemma for service delivery in child sexual abuse;
   (b) to more effectively support their staff;
   (c) to provide peer support.

3. *Specific objectives*
   (a) To have better-informed management, enabling efficient and effective use of resources;
   (b) to provide better staff support—this could be manifested in lower staff turnover, higher staff morale, and improved service delivery;
   (c) to facilitate interagency working at management level.

4. *Limitations*

There is no intention to transform managers into practitioners.

5. *Prerequisites*

None.

The managers who designed a course for practitioners responded to the questions of the exercise as follows:

1. *Aims of course*
   (a) to increase knowledge regarding the range of treatment options available for the treatment of sexually abused children and their families;
   (b) to distinguish between these options and select appropriate cases for treatment.

2. *Learning outcomes*
   (a) to provide an overall framework within which individual treatment programmes could fit.

3. *Specific objectives*
   (a) treatment planning;
   (b) more effective use of existing organizational structures, specifically key workers and case conferences;
   (c) planned treatment interventions;
   (d) better record-keeping;
   (e) recognition of the need to evaluate treatment work.

4. *Limitations*

The course does not develop the necessary therapeutic skills.

5. *Prerequisites*
   (a) foundation course on child sexual abuse;
   (b) multi-disciplinary training for practitioners.

The actual courses they designed are not as important as the material each group presented to each other. Practitioners thought management should be concerned with structures for staff support, whilst managers felt practitioners should concentrate on service delivery. The courses are not mutually exclusive, and had there been time in the small groups it might have been possible for each small group to comment on the course designed for them.

The exercise was designed to provide feedback, to highlight differences constructively within this group, and to reflect areas of concern that were generalizable outside the training experience. As the small groups were made up of professionals from all over the country, none of whom worked together or came from the same agency, the focus of each course was broad but reflected shared preoccupations. By asking the groups to design courses for somebody else, the exercise also promoted an appreciation of difference.

Using natural splits or subgroups within a learning system creatively increases the learning potential for the whole group. For a more homogeneous group, difference can be introduced by using the hypothetical "other".

For example, if practitioners have identified issues they think management should consider in furthering better service delivery, it can be helpful to ask the group to then think what management would identify as being necessary to improve service delivery if they were here. If courses are run in series throughout horizontal slices of the organization, it can be useful to ask each level of the organization what they think another level might say and then compare the lists hypothetically generated with the lists that are actually generated. This gives an indication of the fit within the organization. Is there a shared corporate identity? How in tune are management with the preoccupations of their staff, and vice versa?

Whilst many training packages in child protection have a wealth of training exercises, they are usually designed as if every training group was the same. Experienced trainers know that something that works with one group can go dramatically flat with another.

Thinking about the design and timing of exercises, the balance of input, and the opportunity to establish consensus as well as explore differences in relation to a specific learning system are the skills required of systemic trainers. This involves listening to the feedback the training group is giving throughout the programme and demonstrating a flexibility and creativity in adapting material appropriately such that new learning can take place. It also highlights the importance of process as well as content. It is this process variable that is difficult to describe in training packages. If the whole of a training experience is seen as a process of learning to learn together as a group—with an ideal of transferring this learning experience into learning to work together effectively—then the exercises designed to enhance the learning process could most usefully be viewed as interventions to the learning system. As such they need to be:

(a)   designed for specific training groups, which requires trainers to be flexible enough to modify the exercises they had already planned or those suggested in the training package being used;

(b)   sensitively delivered, to encourage a co-operative response from the learning system which includes providing a rationale for the exercise;

(c)   soliciting feedback regarding the exercise either directly or through observations of the learning system, and giving feedback to participants about their performance of the exercise;

(d)   connected to hypotheses the trainer may have about why this course is happening within this group at this time.

In this way, any training programme moves toward a situation of co-learning and co-evolution such that new information for both the trainer and the trainee can be added to their stochastic storehouse (Whiffen & Byng-Hall, 1982) of child protection skills, and that consolidation of new material occurs recursively for both parties (Keeney, 1983).

CHAPTER SEVEN

Recurring themes and continuous developments in training

The aim of this book was to be long enough to cover the subject but short enough to create interest. I have tried to apply systemic concepts to the field of training specifically in child protection. Training is seen as the intersection of a number of phenomenological domains and as a multi-levelled intervention into or across organizations. Additionally, it is often viewed as the solution to wider problems within and across agencies involved in child protection work. It can be recommended by government inquiries, prescribed because of new legislation, or offered as a means of continuing professional development.

Clearly training lends itself to systemic principles such as co-evolution where reciprocal relationships between trainer and participants develop over time around particular themes. At its best this reciprocity should push all participants, including the trainer, to "the edge of what languaged experience reveals—involving both in the formulation of what has not been said or thought before" (Goolishian & Winderman, 1988, p. 140).

Each training group or event comes together to form a learning system. To do so requires the establishment of boundaries and hierarchy, to help maintain the learning context or matrix of meaning. Because many learning systems are ephemeral and the individual's allegiances are primarily to other systems, the responsibility for setting boundaries rests with the trainer(s). This, in turn, both establishes hierarchy and implicitly confers the role of executive to the trainer(s). To be in the executive position implies a greater degree of responsibility, and also the power to define or set the context within which learning can take place. Consequently, the responsible exercise of authority should be in evidence throughout the duration of the training event.

For child protection professionals, this is a powerful theme because sexual abuse is so completely enmeshed with the abusive use of power both within the family and also in the wider system's response to it. Despite this common knowledge, very few training programmes concentrate on this theme or specifically design exercises that might highlight this. [Exceptions to this are an exercise in Prevention through Protection which specifically focuses on authority issues (Bartlett, 1991) and a training package by OCDS (Goudge & Hori, 1991) which proposes a power model for understanding not only sexual abuse but also other forms of institutionalized oppression.]

Systemic trainers are attuned to the feedback they receive from the participants. Post-course evaluations will not benefit the group who wrote them, but they do perhaps provide a way for individual participants to voice something they were unable to say in the larger group. Feedback in a systemic sense, though, is what you see and hear in the present (Campbell et al., 1991). Trainers can usefully encourage feedback about the training as it is happening, and then adjust material so that the fit between trainer and participants is good enough both to establish consensus and to explore difference. Some training events will also provide the trainer and participants with feedback regarding the wider systems that child protection professionals are connected to. The training context is sufficiently removed from the day-to-day pressures of working life that there is at least a possibility for observing patterns and recognizing what may prove to be unresolvable differences in agency agendas and priorities.

Within the training event, decision making may be explored around complex issues in professional practice, but, at a process

level, there is the tension between encouraging individual responsibility and promoting collective ownership that will make establishing a decision-making mechanism for the course itself
more problematic, especially over short courses. On the whole, the
decisions about the shape of the course and its content will be made
by the trainer with input from the participants. This reinforces the
systemic trainer's role as executive to the learning system.

Facilitating the development of greater expertise within the training group over time should shift the differential of expertise from
trainer to trainee. If learning is taking place, the possibility for a
more equal distribution should begin to emerge. Clearly, this is
more likely to occur in training programmes that run over time.
This pattern of nurturance without fostering life-long dependence is
especially difficult to achieve. It is a pattern that occurs in many
contexts other than the training arena, but one that frequently
impacts on the training experience. Professional workers in child
protection repeatedly refer to the stresses they experience as a
consequence of their work. They often feel they do not receive
the supervision they should, and they use training events as an
opportunity to be fed both intellectually as well as emotionally. This
may be equally true for the trainer.

Training needs to recognize this aspect of the work and
help professionals identify the right forum in which to raise
their concerns. If training is isolated and set apart from the wider
organization, it will reinforce the feelings of impotence and dis-
connectedness that the professionals are expressing. In this way,
training can become the organization's conflict-regulating mechanisms. It can be used to siphon-off complaints about lack of
supervision and a shortfall in resources by implying that greater
knowledge and skills is the problem.

Training can be used as the bridge for the implementation
gap between policy and practice. It can also be used to bridge the
gender gap in child protection between predominantly male
management and predominantly female practitioners. To be more
effective at doing so, training should occur not only in horizontal
slices of the organization but also vertical ones. This would enable
different levels of the system to interact in a different context and to
elaborate the feedback vital to competent functioning that is so
often attenuated due to pressure of work. Levels of organizations

disconnected from each other, or agencies who have no way of communicating with each other, will be unable to deal with the inevitable crisis that child protection work will generate.

The design of courses as a whole should begin to reflect the need to actively promote positive transfer of training skills to the work context. To do this, management needs to be fully engaged in the task of selection, not only of individuals for training, but also of courses. This should be wedded to the overall agency plan of action, in which priority learning tasks can be identified along with priority target audiences. Whilst evaluation of courses themselves may be useful, it is also important to see training generating change in the professional practice of participants. The Department of Health Training Programme in Child Sexual Abuse (chapter two) has continued to evolve. Every intake, of which there have been four to date, has been slightly different from the previous intake. This is an example of a training programme learning to learn from itself. The course aims to actively promote positive transfer of training, not only for an individual trainee, but also for the organization that nominates the trainee on the programme, by encouraging the Development Group that contains a vertical slice of the child protection network to consume the course with the aim of specific service developments for the nominating authority.

Over time the course has retained its original four-component structure: academic, clinical, training, and organizational. The rationale for the range of components is to touch on all aspects of the adult learning cycle of thinking, feeling, and doing and to put professional practice into its organizational context. The balance has shifted from training an individual to training an identified group of individuals who represent different levels within and between organizations.

Development Groups not only contain key players within organizations who might facilitate change, but also actively use these professionals in the programme itself. This reinforces the message that working together is helpful and necessary in child protection. It also tries to encourage structural changes within organizations that will protect, develop, and extend service developments in the long run.

In running this programme and writing this book, I have had the unique opportunity of testing out many of the ideas described.

Some of these attempts are documented in the case material. By viewing training itself systemically, I have found that I do not become bored with teaching the same material, because each training experience is different. It represents a new learning system which may have some of the same needs as previous ones, but almost certainly will also have different ones.

I can remember running what were supposed to be identical workshops for an organization; one was for women only, the other for a mixed audience of men and women. Some women wanted to attend both because they did not understand why the organizers had asked me to run two separate programmes. The courses, whilst dealing with the same material, were different. They differed in atmosphere, the questions asked, and the areas focused on. The women who attended both workshops experienced that difference and felt that they had a better understanding as to why some of their women colleagues did not wish to attend a mixed male–female training event on sexual abuse. The same training material taught by the same trainer but with different audiences generated totally different learning systems.

Systemic training probably requires the trainer to be connected to and enthusiastic about their training material. However, this does not mitigate against maintaining a neutrality about it (Boston & Draper, 1985). An approach that encourages an interactional style, a degree of flexibility, and a capacity to modify or create exercises on the spot relies on a firm grasp of both the theoretical material and systemic techniques. Training others often is an indication of an individual having reached a level of competence where the challenge of explaining to others what you think you know about a particular subject is viewed as enjoyable.

Training groups help trainers reflect on their own learning. The clarity I have developed in my work over the years is, in part, due to the inquisitiveness of the participants at the many training events I have done. Yet I realise that this clarity can be unhelpful. It can result in participants feeling unable to achieve a level of competence, and it can appear to be dogmatic. If I do not, as a trainer, connect onto what trainees already know, then it is unlikely that the foundation will have been laid for new learning to take place.

Cultivating areas of incompetence is a skill that I am acquiring. This coupled with saying no and using the three stranger questions from the *Feeling Yes, Feeling No* child protection training programme (Van Riesen, undated) [Do I have a yes or no feeling about this training event? Does someone I trust know where I am? Can I get help if I need it? If you get a no answer to any of these questions, don't train alone] forms part of my professional self-protection plan. It also demonstrates that it can be useful to practise what you teach.

APPENDIX

Department of Health
Postgraduate Training in Child Sexual Abuse

The Department of Health Postgraduate Training Programme has had four intakes to date. This summary gives information about all four intakes. The intakes have become progressively smaller and more uni-disciplinary. The programme was intended to be multi-disciplinary and multi-agency.

Figure A looks at trainees by discipline for all four intakes. Social workers have clearly been in the majority since the inception of the programme. More detailed consideration has been given to the recruitment of Health Service staff onto this programme. The majority of trainees have been female, 26 of 30, and white, 28 of 30.

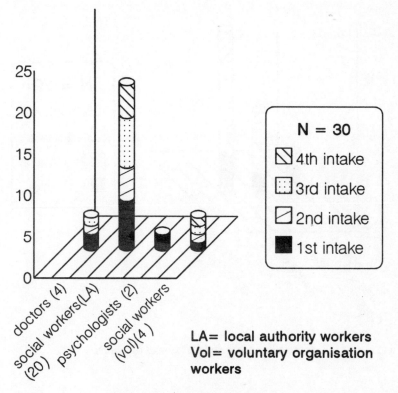

N = 30
◻ 4th intake
⊞ 3rd intake
◩ 2nd intake
■ 1st intake

doctors (4)
social workers(LA) (20)
psychologists (2)
social workers (vol)(4)

LA= local authority workers
Vol= voluntary organisation workers

Figure A: Trainees by discipline

Figure B indicates the geographical spread of trainees. Only 29 trainees are considered in this particular table, as one trainee on the fourth intake was not consuming the whole of the programme but attending for the academic programme only. The programme has been singularly unsuccessful in recruiting any nominations from the northwest of England. However, we have been successful in securing nominations from as far away as Newcastle and Cornwall. In the fourth intake only, we have solicited applications from voluntary organizations. Members from voluntary organizations attend the programme on behalf of the whole of their organization. They are not required to be connected to an Area Child Protection Committee but to have full managerial backing of central headquarters of their organization.

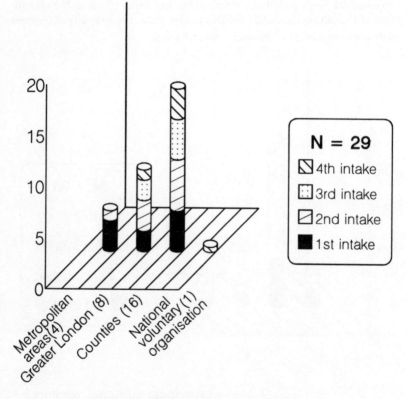

Figure B: Geographical spread of trainees

REFERENCES

Armstrong, H., & Hollows, A. (1989a). *What's in the Box: Evaluations of Training Materials in Child Sexual Abuse.* London: National Children's Bureau.

Armstrong, H., & Hollows, A. (1989b). *A Positive Model: Standards for the Development and Evaluation of Material for Training in Child Sexual Abuse.* London: National Children's Bureau.

Bartlett, R. (Ed.) (1991). *Protection Through Prevention: Child Protection—A Programme of Interdisciplinary Staff Development.* Cheshire: Changing Perspectives.

Beckford Report (1985). *A Child in Trust: A Report of the Panel of Inquiry into the Circumstances the Death of Jasmine Beckford.* London: Borough of Brent.

Benson, J. K. (1975). The interorganisational network as a political economy. *Administrative Science Quarterly. 20*: 229–249.

Borthwick, S. (1991). From victims to survivors. *Social Work Today* (12 September).

Boston, P., & Draper, R. (1985). When learning is the problem. In: D. Campbell & R. Draper (Eds.), *Applications of Systemic Family Therapy: The Milan Approach* (pp. 249–258). London: Grune & Stratton.

Burnham, J. (1986). *Family Therapy.* London: Tavistock Publications.

Byrne, K., & Patrick, N. (1990). Bexley bounces back. *Social Work Today* (20 April).

Campbell, D., Draper, R., & Huffington, C. (1991). *A Systemic Approach to Consultation*. London: Karnac Books.

Caswell, R. (1987). Towards non-sexist family therapy. *South West Region Women and Family Therapy Group* (June).

Charles, M., & Stevenson, O. (1990). *Multi-Disciplinary Is Different: Child Protection: Working Together. Part 1. The Process of Learning and Training. Part 2. Sharing Perspectives*. Nottingham: University of Nottingham.

Cleveland Report (1988). *Report of the Inquiry into Child Abuse in Cleveland in 1987*. CM412. London: HMSO.

Clyde, Lord (1992). *The Report of the Inquiry into the Removal of Children in Orkney in February 1991*. Edinburgh: HMSO.

Cronen, V., Pearce, B., & Tomm, K. (1985). A dialectical view of personal change. In: K. Gergen & K. Davis (Eds.), *The Social Construction of the Person* (pp. 203–224). New York: Springer-Verlag.

Cross, T. (1991). *On Developing Cultural Competence*. Workshop presented at The Excellence in Training Conference, Cornell University, July.

Curry, D., Caplan, P., & Knupple (1991). *Transfer of Training and Adult Learning*. North East Ohio Regional Training Centre.

Davies, E., Kidd, L., & Pringle, K. (1987). *Child Sexual Abuse Training Programme for Foster Parents with Teenage Placements*. Newcastle: Barnardo's Family Placement Project. North East Division.

Department of Health and Social Security (1982). *Child Abuse: A Study of Inquiry Report*. London: HMSO.

Department of Health and Social Security (1988). *Working Together: A Guide to Arrangements for Inter-Agency Co-operation for the Protection of Children from Abuse*. London: HMSO.

Department of Health Social Services Inspectorate (1990). *Inspection of Child Protection Services in Rochdale*. Manchester: DHSSI, North West Region.

Department of Health (1991a). *Working with Child Sexual Abuse: Guidelines for Trainers and Managers in Social Service Departments*. London: HMSO.

Department of Health (1991b). *Working Together under The Children Act 1989*. London: HMSO.

Donnelly, P. (1992). Against the grain. *Community Care* (25 June), pp. 5–6.

Ducanis, A. J., & Golin, A. K. (1979). The interdisciplinary health care team, Germantown, MD, Aspens Systems Corporation. In: C. Hallett & E. Birchall (Eds.), *Co-ordination and Child Protection: A Review of the Literature*. London: HMSO.

Furniss, T. (1983). Mutual influence: interlocking professionals—family process in treatment of child sexual abuse and incest. *Child Abuse & Neglect. 7* (2): 207–223.

Georgiades, N., & Phillimore, L. (1975). The myth of the hero innovator and alternative strategies for organisational change. In: C. C. Kiernan & F. Woodford (Eds.), *Behaviour Modification in the Severely Retarded*. Amsterdam: Association Scientific Publishers.

Goldner, V. (1991). Feminism and systemic practice: Two critical traditions in transition. *Journal of Family Therapy. 13*: 95–104.

Goolishian, H., & Winderman, L. (1988). Constructivism, autotopoiesis and problem-determined systems. *The Irish Journal of Psychology, 9* (1): 130–143.

Goudge, P., & Hori, A. (1991). *Child Sexual Abuse and Racism*. Sheffield: Organisational & Social Development Consultants, 355 Fullwood Road, S10 3BQ.

Hallett, C., & Birchall, E. (1992). *Co-ordination and Child Protection: A Review of the Literature*. London: HMSO.

Hollows, A., Stainton-Rogers, W., & Armstrong, H. (1989). *Good Enough Training: Managing and Developing Training in Child Sexual Abuse. Managers' Pack and Trainers' Pack*. Newport Pagnell: Learning Materials Design.

Imber-Black, E. (1988). *Families in Larger Systems: A Family Therapist's Guide through the Labyrinth*. London: Guildford Press.

Keeney, B. (1983). *The Aesthetics of Change*. London: Guilford Press.

Kelly, L. (1988). *Surviving Sexual Violence*. Cambridge: Polity Press.

Kelly, L., & Regan, L. (1990). Flawed protection. *Social Work Today, 21* (32): 13–15.

Metropolitan Police & Bexley Social Services (1987). *Child Sexual Abuse: Joint Investigative Programme: Bexley Experiment: Final Report*. London: HMSO.

Morin, B. N. (1982). *Science avec conscience*. Paris: Fayard.

Morrison, T. (1990). *The Emotional Effects of Child Protection Work on the Worker*. Paper presented at the BASPCAN Spring Conference (April).

Napier, A. Y., & Whittaker, C. (1978). *The Family Crucible*. Cambridge. MA: Harvard University Press.

Paul, D. (1977). Sexual examination and variation of the hymen. *Police Surgeon. 11*: 19–41.

Selvini-Palazzoli, M., Boscolo, L., Cecchin, G., & Prata, G. (1980a). Hypothesizing–circularity–neutrality: three guidelines for the conductor of the session. *Family Process. 19* (1): 3–12.

Selvini-Palazzoli, M., Cirillo, S., Selvini, M., & Sorrentino, A. (1989). *Family Games: General Modes of Psychotic Processes in the Family.* London: Karnac Books.

Senge, P. (1990). *The Fifth Discipline: The Art and Practice of the Learning Organization.* New York: Doubleday.

Smith, G. (1979). Rape and forensic practice. *The Police Surgeon. 16*: 46–56.

Smith, G. (1991). *Working Together to Protect and Empower Victims.* Paper presented at The Regional Offenders Treatment Association Conference.

Van Riesen, W. (undated). *Feeling Yes, Feeling No, A Sexual Assault Prevention Programme for Young Children: A Guide.* Produced by the National Film Board of Canada, Pacific Region. Printed by The National Clearing House on Family Violence, Health and Welfare, Canada. Distributed in the United Kingdom by Educational Media International.

Warner (1992). *Choosing with Care. The Report of the Committee of Inquiry into the Selection, Development and Management of Staff in Children's Homes.* London: HMSO.

Whiffen, R., & Byng-Hall, J. (1982). *Family Therapy Supervision: Recent Developments in Practice.* London: Academic Press.